DISTURB / ENRAPTURE

ASSARACUS
A JOURNAL OF GAY AND QUEER POETRY

27

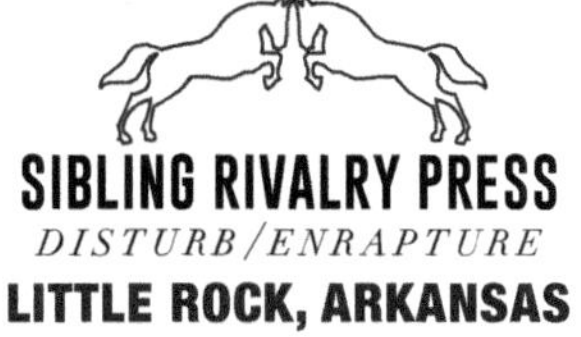

SIBLING RIVALRY PRESS
DISTURB/ENRAPTURE
LITTLE ROCK, ARKANSAS

Cover image: "Drag King at Cake Bar on Avenue B, 1996" by Efrain John Gonzalez. Used with permission.

I stumbled upon this issue's cover photograph when, at the urging of Perry Brass, I visited Efrain John Gonzalez's exhibition *Public Places, Secret Spaces* at the SoHo Project Space at 127 Prince Street in NYC in September 2025. Efrain's work showcases his truthful, candid, and intimate black-and-white images of the 1970s–90s NYC scene, particularly the sex piers, the drag scene, and local queer and underground life. He gave me a personal tour and told stories about each photograph as we walked through the gallery. So many of his photos leapt out at me, and it was clear from his work and his memories that he has a long, supportive history with queer poetry. I knew the cover image I wanted the moment I saw it, and he allowed me to purchase it for use. Now I call him a friend, and he sends me photos he takes throughout each week. He's a beautiful human. I love the people art has brought into my life.

Sibling Rivalry Press
159 Sunset Drive
North Little Rock, AR 72118
info@siblingrivalrypress.com
www.siblingrivalrypress.com

Printed in the United States of America.

Founding Editor: Bryan Borland
www.bryanborland.com

ISBN: 978-1-943977-89-5
ISSN: 2159-0478

Assaracus Issue 27: A Journal of Gay and Queer Poetry
January 2026.

REPEAT AFTER ME:

**IF YOU ARE NOT QUEER
QUEER POETRY
IS NOT YOUR
SAFE SPACE.
YOU ARE WELCOME
BUT YOUR COMFORT
IS NOT OUR PRIORITY.**

**OUR JOY IS.
OUR SEX IS.
OUR ART IS.
OUR LIVES ARE.
OUR SURVIVAL IS.**

COVER PHOTOGRAPH

DRAG KING AT CAKE BAR
on AVENUE B, 1996

EFRAIN JOHN GONZALEZ

EFRAIN JOHN GONZALEZ IS A PHOTOGRAPHIC ARTIST WHOSE TALENTS WITH CAMERA AND DARKROOM HAVE ALLOWED HIM TO DOCUMENT AND PUBLISH THE WILD AND CRAZY NIGHTLIFE OF NEW YORK CITY'S UNDERGROUND CLUB AND FETISH PARTY SCENE. HE HAD UNIQUE ACCESS TO SOME OF THE KINKIEST AND OVER THE TOP EVENTS THAT WERE POPPING UP ALL OVER THE OLD MEAT PACKING DISTRICT WHEN IT WAS STILL FULL OF RED MEAT.
FOR MORE = **WWW.HELLFIREPRESS.COM**

FEATURING

LOVES OF MY LIFE

I want to use every page of *Assaracus* to support the queer arts community. Here's a list of **loves of my life** lately; you might love them, too.

BOOK: *Outliving Michael* by Steven Reigns (Moon Tide Press) is a devastating, luminous masterpiece. It's an intimate, clear-eyed elegy in which Reigns resurrects a lost friend with such tenderness and precision that the book feels less like reading poems and more like being granted the privilege of witnessing a life restored to light.

FILM: *Fairyland* is a gorgeously tender coming-of-age film that transforms Alicia Abbott's memoir of the same name into a shimmering love letter to being imperfectly human, capturing the ache, beauty, and fragile wonder of growing up with, and ultimately grieving, a father (gay poet Steve Abbott) whose life burned brightly against the backdrop of a changing, complicated America. Bonus points for scattering issues of *Gay Sunshine* in various shots.

POET: C. Dale Young is one of the rare poets whose work feels at once surgically precise and incandescently human. He's a writer who can cut straight to the bone with a single line and then flood the wound with light. Don't miss his *Building the Perfect Animal: New and Selected Poems* from Four Way Books.

PRESS: Green Linden Press has something special in the works. Launching in January 2026, *Salon des Refusés* is its new imprint named for an 1863 exhibit of artists rejected from the prestigious Paris Salon, and it will champion projects that, for various reasons, have remained unseen—those deemed too strange, too unmarketable, or those chronically turned down.

SONG: Brandi Carlile's "Returning to Myself" sounds like Joni Mitchell, especially when she sings, "I love you and you and you." After spending much of her time working with legends, it's nice to see some self-love.

THE FUTURE: I'm excited for Emanuel Xavier's *Still, We Are Sacred*, coming in April from Rebel Satori. Justin Torres blurbed it: "A poem can of course be a confrontation; a provocation; a pastoral ode to the wild turkeys of Staten Island; an address to the recreant father; a lament; a love letter; an assertion of dignity.... Xavier delivers on all these fronts, and more, with hard-won honesty and rhythmic urgency."

XOXO // BB

KEVIN BERTOLERO
HOW THE BOYS SMELLED

KEVIN BERTOLERO IS THE FOUNDING EDITOR OF BOTH GHOST CITY PRESS AND *& CHANGE POETRY*. **HE HOLDS DEGREES IN LITERATURE FROM POTSDAM COLLEGE AND THE UNIVERSITY OF NEW HAMPSHIRE, AS WELL AS AN MFA FROM NEW ENGLAND COLLEGE WHERE HE CURRENTLY TEACHES WRITING. KEVIN IS THE AUTHOR OF THREE COLLECTIONS OF POETRY, MOST RECENTLY** *IN PASSING*, **AS WELL AS A NONFICTION BOOK** *FOREVER IN TRANSITION: QUEER FUTURIST AESTHETICS IN GAY CINEMA*. **HIS WORK HAS APPEARED IN OR IS FORTHCOMING WITH** *HANGING LOOSE*, *THE CORTLAND REVIEW*, *POST ROAD*, *BLUELINE MAGAZINE*, *OLNEY MAG*, *FOURTEEN POEMS*, **AND ELSEWHERE. HE LIVES IN PORTLAND, MAINE.**

THE NEW YEAR

for Jack

A photo from last January
on the kitchen table
with your letter from
this past week, that

you were in Missoula again
—wrote how the sunsets are
very different from Dallas

like in a documentary, how
the light comes in from almost
zero angle
and in the room I'm in

—the photo being of this same
room—looks different now.

I love you
—you know that when I
look out at the little brook
in the woods behind

the yard I think you'd
stand there in the water
watching something
                    I could
never see.

SLEEPING SICKNESS

I wake up and put on *La Calda Vita*
—sick on the couch watching
Jacques Perrin peel his shirt off,
only twenty-two but I'd die for him.

Still not morning, though you sit with me
and hug my legs. *Oh, he wants him bad*,
you say, pointing at the screen. Max looks
at Freddi how I know you look at me,

in a way that you can photograph but
you can't just write it down. I saw it last
summer, too—thought I had you on tape.
But I shoot DV so when I play it back

we only get the haze. The things I make,
I make for you, but they're of no origin
—or are beyond me.
Does this make sense to you?

Outside we hear the morning traffic
and you turn down the volume on the TV.
It's almost like their ocean, you tell me.
On the bluff, Freddi looks out at the

Tyrrhenian Sea, bluest sky of Sardinia
above his head. Max watches him from
a distance. When the sun comes up,
you're asleep on me and I can feel your

breathing. Things are so different now.
I've never told you this, but I love the way
you smell, and how after sleeping in
your bed, I also kind of smell like you.

DEVOTIONAL

Sitting with it
while the snow
comes and I think
—how in a
cycle we come
back to center
—are *you* my
center? December
at the Skaneateles
community indoor
pool, all I could do
was compare my size,
how the boys smelled
in the car driving home.
Fell asleep like that,
on your shoulder,
your hair still wet.

TRAVEL

And in July we both
lie naked in your bed
unmoving—do you
think of us like this,
together, swimming
in the Pemi? The wild-
fire haze grows too thick
for us to bother getting
up. How hard it is
to move in this heat.
You are sweating
and, momentarily,
I think I see the man
I thought you were.

IFF / SOMERVILLE

Manfredi Marini in *Diciannove* then dinner at the Burren. It's 7:30 and the night is still light and the after-rain smell, it's everywhere, even at the bar where the windows are open and the students are shouting outside in protest. I haven't felt this high on a new face in a year or more, how everything felt so like me—Leo's books, desire—how a year, or more, feels when you know what you want but not how to get it.

ANOTHER BEAUTIFUL EMPTY ROOM

for Edmund White

In a previous life, I wonder if
this city walk, for you, felt
the same—in the fall when
the port is filled with wind
—how sun pours in through
your studio window, a midday
shadow just as you depart.
Then the quiet when you're
gone which I won't get used to.
There was a theater with a small
marquee and just above it you
loved the way some ivy crawled
the bricks. *Just enough*, you said.
How when the weather clears
you feel more like yourself again.

APRIL

There's this patch of purple shade
on the wall from the window.
I take a photo. It's cold again.

Today I drive downtown to see
Star Garden at the archive and
the theater is one-third full.

When I leave, outside, the light
is receding, like a solar cycle
on that wall beneath the stairs.

There was a house in the North
Country, built next to a cabin which
in winter grew so cold, though

Ginnie kept the fire alive all night.
Can you imagine a summer here,
she asked, and I think of lying

in the day bed next to the field of
clover. Like shadows, I see you turn
the pages of a book, some volume

which you've never seen before.
And the sunlight pours through
the trees, filtered in the window,

again, onto your skin, and makes you
glow. We make a meal like this,
a little quince jam on some toast,

a VHS in the player at night when
our home, and the land behind, are dark—
Brandon de Wilde in *Hud*, so gorgeous.

And when you go up to sleep,
the floorboards creak. I wanted a home
next to the river, but you thought it

too old, and the barn too large. I fill our
empty pots with viny plants and pull off
the leaves when they turn some royal yellow.

An empty chair on the porch waits for you,
how the light looks though the pages of your
book. A poem aloud before bed and we talk

about it. Not what it means but what it makes
you feel. Is this the dream state? Is the picture
window glowing with the coolness of the

summer air, sitting in the shade. A bowl of
cornflakes in the morning, a ripe banana,
another glass of water—

What dissolves in what comes first—
late-spring hail on the little river, or the way
you stand behind me on the sidewalk,

follow me wherever I choose to lead.

ON MOTHER'S DAY

An exception
is made, or
offered—how
on our trip to
town, when you
get your ice
cream cone and
proceed to drop it,
we share mine
instead.
I think of
the last time
we spoke and how
you thought to
bring the tomato
plant inside, to
protect it from
the coastal wind.
A garden
is a delight
to the eye, and
—despite the
coldness of
these nights
—a solace
for the soul.
How I desire,
still, another
nap with you
as our window
shades shift
in the breeze,
the glowing
multitude,
those squares
of light.

A KINDNESS

This could be a day of release—
a dam floods the territory,
as scheduled, alarms sound
(I think of Jia's Three Gorges)
—and on the opposite shore
I see myself writing a poem
for you that I should have
written years before. Sorry it
took so long. I'm finding every
morning is another shower to
wash away our sweat, the cum,
and you just laugh. Only two
months ago, we were walking
Boothbay and the heat was crushing.
Sometimes I think I'm unwell,
but how do you account for that?
In my room is a stack of books
you look at every time you
visit. On the ferry to Monhegan,
you've brought one with you,
just to think on it. Name a
two-word phrase that makes
me laugh; I dare you. A couple
Coors and sunburnt knees by the
time we dock—one disposable
camera keeps clicking, though the
film is destined for underdevelopment.
You read me a line from "Hymn
to Life" and out the window I see
the steps leading up to the house
on Manana. Schuyler means so
much to me, and now, I guess,
to you. I want my friends
to be friends—in fact, that's
all I want.

CONCISION

A photo of young James Merrill
& you can feel the pricks of light
—imperfect thirty-five
—the curl of his hair. He once
woke up on a farm in Vermont &
wrote about the feeling for which
he knew of no return—rising to a
man you only *think* you love,   or
maybe it's real?   Oh, to be
a different person—a toiler,
a wayfarer. Consider Jimmy's letters
from Great Spruce Head, a total loss.
Or a PennSound playlist, group
reading of *Flow Chart* & I can't
stop myself—*what is going on here?*
Sometimes, I feel the boat sway
& like a Wyeth, I am adrift. At the
museum in Ogunquit we see a
Cudahy, his "Blue, Blue Room,"
in which the windows are open
& the painter's in the mirror.
Two men on the floor clutching
Madonna lilies & it's the end of day,
I think. Imagine knowing *why*
you're like this. Imagine being—
for someone else—that shining future
you cannot see.

THERESA DAVIS
RING YOURSELF AWAKE

THERESA DAVIS IS AN AWARD-WINNING POET, EDUCATOR, AND CAFFEINE-POWERED WORD WIZARD BASED IN ATLANTA, GEORGIA. KNOWN FOR SETTING MICROPHONES ON FIRE (METAPHORICALLY... MOSTLY), THERESA BLENDS HUMOR, HEART, AND A HINT OF REBELLION IN EVERY VERSE. HER BOOKS INCLUDE *AFTER THIS WE GO DARK* **AND** *DROWNED: A MERMAID'S MANIFESTO***, BOTH FROM SIBLING RIVALRY PRESS AND INCLUDED ON THE AMERICAN LIBRARY ASSOCIATION'S** *OVER THE RAINBOW* **LIST OF RECOMMENDED LGBTQ READING. SHE IS ALSO A FORMER WOMEN OF THE WORLD POETRY SLAM CHAMPION. WHEN SHE'S NOT TEACHING THE NEXT GENERATION OF POETS OR GRACING STAGES WITH HER FIERCE PERFORMANCES, SHE'S PROBABLY KILLING HER PLANTS OR PLOTTING THE NEXT GREAT HAIKU ABOUT SWEET TEA AND SOCIAL JUSTICE. THE NAME OF THIS SEQUENCE,** *RING YOURSELF AWAKE***, FROM THE POEM "INHERITANCE," IS A PERMANENT NEON BEACON AT THE GOAT FARM IN ATLANTA.**

A PEP TALK 'CAUSE MY SKIN IS TIRED!

Sistas!

Listen,

sometimes you have to step back,
because every fight ain't yours—
& this tea is delicious.

You're not hanging up
on the fight,
you're just hanging out
with yourself,
staying hydrated & shyt!

No point getting worked up
over mess we didn't create—
the same mess we've been
working through since we got here.

Girl, go to the gym,
do some
Hot Ass Yoga!!

Because,
you deserve everything you desire—
and right now that means sweat!

And sometimes,

you have to let your cute loose.
Get your nails did.
Get your wig snatched.
Beat your face and saunter your cute everywhere.
Strap on those heels,
embrace your inner everything,
and
STRUT!

Listen,
you deserve your peace of mind.
Your emotional labor is your own.
And you, my sista,
are phucking amazing!
The only thing you owe anyone
is to stay healthy, happy, hydrated,
and alive!

WE SHOULDN'T, BUT WE ARE

If you were everything I needed,
I would not be writing this now.
I was just trying to have a conversation with you—
but it was about art,
and you don't do art.

Then it was about politics, but you don't do politics.
It was about me wanting to take you out on a date,
do something other than fuck for a change.

I say theater,
you say movie.
I say play,
you say I don't do plays.
I ask why—
which seems to be the code word for distract me,
rubbing up against my soft parts,
taking advantage of my sexual ADHD,
and suddenly we are fucking again.

You are letting me.
I am letting you.
Belts are breaking,
beds are breaking,
then you are passed out,
and I am laid up next to you,
writing a poem
about how I don't need to be with you.

And the distance between us
is farther than it appears—
close enough for fingers to stroke,
but never close enough to meet in the mind,
'cause you don't do that.

I can't have a conversation
with you without a drink in my throat,
because it is the only way you made sense.
And the distance between us is addiction—

we crave the separateness like alcoholics
craving a fifth of whatever's cheapest,
our soil so saturated we will not settle.

You want my touch less than I want to give it to you,
and this is how we've stuck ourselves
into an existence neither of us will walk away from,
because we don't know how.
We know we are not who we used to be.

The best thing about us is bottom beauty and strap-ons—
and because I am a hopeless romantic and you are lazy,
the way we lie, it is almost believable. Almost.

Soon there will be nothing left to anchor us.
We are going to crash and burn and drown,
and I don't imagine you reaching out
or throwing me a life preserver.
Why would you save me
when you couldn't save yourself from me?

This shine we've put on this shitty relationship
should shame us both. And the fact that I am
in bed with you, listening to you snore,
writing a poem that you will never read
because you don't do art,
makes me realize how blind we are to the reality
that we actually don't like each other.

I love you like a root canal is not sexy.
Neither is I love you like an exit wound.
We are sick—in need of a twelve-step program,
one where we walk away from each other,
slowly at first,
then run like hell and never look back.

When you told me you loved me,
I was splayed beneath you, all moan and cum.
I wasn't even wearing my charm.
And I noticed:
you never loved me with my clothes on.

TONSORIAL

When you are a single mother
with three boys
who have hair
that they refuse to comb,
and school starts soon,

you know there are stores that sell clippers,
so you buy a pair.
The barber shop is expensive—
three visits pays for the clippers.

Then,

there is more money
for the clothes they are outgrowing,
for the shoes that always need replacing,
for the meals missing midday in summer.

This practical single mother knows
she has no skills at cutting hair,
but how hard can it be?
She has seen hair cut.

Her sons are not eager to be
experimental performance art.
No one wants to go first.
The youngest loses the fight
because
Youngest.

He sits not as calm as he pretends.
There is a soft buzz,
an ouch,
a retort of
"damn, your ears are big,"
a little blood,
then

oops.

The older brother slaps his hand
across his lips
to stuff back the expletive
that will get his ass beat.
The sisters laugh on the stairs.

The younger brother advances on
the mirror,
mouth stretched in a scream
that won't come.
A tear falls.

The mother is upset.
She didn't do it on purpose.
She apologizes to the crying boy
who now has to have it

all

cut

off.

A trim turned scalping.
The older brother declares
he wants to grow the biggest
afro in the world.
Ever.

The middle son takes to grooming
like it's his newfound religion,
while the younger son develops
an interest
in hats.

The clippers find a new home in a drawer,
away from shaking hands,
its job done

until school begins again.

INHERITANCE

Born in smoke and salt,
a gift given despite drought
and questionable choices—
grandmother discarded,
waste spanning decades.
A dead tree
in a yard of dead trees.
No one asked;
no one answered.
Another block,
sand everywhere.

I release you—
the smoke holding your breath,
the rock burdening your good heart
lifted under wobbling legs.
Give it away.
Make your arms open,
a bell—
ring yourself awake.

She had no idea he would return,
the gift of watered-down love
exactly how he received it:
without the fanfare of beards,
ignored abuse
scorching his retreating feet.

He dug her grave so long ago,
he forgot where he left her.
No one is willing to pick up the mantle.
Passed away,
the prize returned to the dust
from which it was born.

THE VIGIL

Before Interment

The day the air stopped working—
dead screens, team spirit,
arms wrapped exactly as I found them,
hands tucked into hymns,
palms empty, moving all around.
A soundtrack of silence,
a variable with no value
multiplied by itself,
solutions hanging,
a backdrop of unsent prayers,
timelines with unwanted guests.

The hope inside all that sadness—
the years peeling, a shedding of skin;
leaves leaping to their deaths,
flashes of orange and red.
I was always holding the camera,
never in the picture.

A stinging ocean swims up my throat,
collapses my lungs; my feet, rooted
and stubborn, do not fall.
The word sweetheart lost in the echo,
pretense on repeat;
the air so thin
I forgot my own name for months.

The leaving makes the sugar.
I remember the sweet in spring—
lungs full, but the sweet left.
I had to.
I had to let it go.
Thought I was holding substance,
not a clutch of lies.
Clear the house, rid myself of the clutter;
sweep the dirt out the door;
finally eat a meal that could hold me.

I've been feasting on famine,
desensitized to the hunger pains
that rack my body midday,
remind me I am living and alive
and starving to death—
a strange circumstance,
a pause in the beat and break,
an apology never received or accepted,
a buffet awaiting my devouring.
I am windswept
and passion,
and I am so tired.

I have etched the word love into my palms,
to the point of infection—
a hiccup in the lifeline.
But I refuse to hold them up in surrender,
and you don't want to know any of this.

It looks too much like open wounds and bleeding out,
all teeth and hair and a scream trapped—
something meant to be secret or silent,
even though my eyes don't hide much.

I miss swimming in summer,
letting go and falling away
from preconceived notions;
holding myself close and others accountable;
prepared to take the next steps—
even if it looks like falling,
or love lifting.
Even if it's not real—
I mean, it could be.

THE VERDICT

A word to the wind
that did not stir—
not a breeze.

A coward capable of sight,
refusing to see;
her blindfold never moved.

What do we do now, brother wind?

What kind of freedom can you offer
to those who are not seen by justice,
still
murdered for the loudness of their Black?

What protection can you offer to wildflower
bouquets—
handcuffed, then wrapped in
plastic the color of body bags?

Did you not hear my questions, brother wind?
Are you holding your breath?
Should we hold ours too,
or do we wait?

Let their gavels bang our dead bodies to dust,
scattered in the dirt,
our ghosts left to be tried for our murders.

Will you exhale then, brother wind?
Scatter our remains in safer soil,
where people are not born
to die.

MEANWHILE

In the meantime,
the air still chills the bite,
tempting scarves and sweaters
from their summer strongholds.
It is rude and disrespectful.

The breeze, a sudden cool,
attempts to steal your breath
as fall protests its lack of stage time.
The streets—mostly empty—
a pleasant change from
what seems to be constant
rush hour.

Leftovers
becoming sides,
becoming soups,
if the weather holds.

The bustle
soon to return
in splashes of red and green—
a poinsettia for every table.

There are holidays
I do not acknowledge.
This is one of them.

Once I learned the definition of colonization—
the only true invention of white-ness—
stealing,
possessing,
enslaving
everything Black or Brown.
A particular cruelty groomed over time.
The way the term has changed,
not the skintone,
into words like
founding

and gentrify.
When you know that habit of horror,
the notion
of inviting
an unknown,
a white entity,
into your home
and offering it
cookies
sounds like the beginning
of a bad day for decades.

In the meantime,
I survey my yard,
consider if I could grow
my own food,
wonder if I'd get the hang of it
before it is deemed illegal;
consider if the soil can fortify;
consider what was buried there before—
seeds knowing america is a graveyard,
above and below the ground.

LITANY OR PITFALLS AND PROBABILITY

You can see it in her eyes—
the way they slip in and out of focus,
the lazy blink as if in disbelief,
the pyrotechnics of her thoughts
playing back in real time.
She knows she won't last. How could she,
when she is walking around in the world
with all that dark skin
and the wrong god?

Is today the day her world shifts so swiftly
she is thrown off-kilter
and away at the same time?
The dirt beneath her feet barely stirs dust,
because we all know, in this America,
first ladies are not a favorite
in any color other than white.

Will she find out when we do—
on a screen in our hands or on walls?
Will she see when we do
the first cracks of infidelity?

Will it be on a murky Monday,
after a weekend of starving children,
when the words fly from his mouth?
Will it be with words,
or will it be actions?

Will it be a filthy Friday,
the news full of kidnapping and cruelty,
full of masked men and empty bellies?

Will we catch the cover-up before it starts?
Will it be scandalous or respectable
when he turns to comfort another woman,
her hand tangled all up in his hair—
mourning free and fresh in Christian leather pants,
looking for love in the whitest of houses?

INHERITANCE: AFTER THE EXHUMATION

The walls, like I have been holding our breath;
the slide of scales, weight released over decades.
My memories stretch across canvas,
the smell of paint perfuming the air.

When my words won't come,
I retreat to glue and turpentine—
the snip of scissors, acrylics, and oil.
There are places I can escape from
in plain sight,
make it a destination,
a remembrance eagerly received.

In the days before today,
when basement confinement
was her idea of child care
or cover-up—
no sugar for the tea,
the stale scent of dank, dark dirt filling my nose—

back then, my arsenal for exodus
was limited to crayons missing their tips,
markers afraid to show their bold,
their tops covered in teeth marks—
not mine.

I would draw a world
where there were no basements,
all the tea had sugar.

In that world, she cares more for her grandchildren
than her son's cheating lovers;
more than being the prettiest beard;
more than being a friend
instead of a mother to a son who will discard her—
teaching lessons that should not be learned.
In that world, I see her future,
know her son will find her a basement of her own.

I wonder if he apologized
before planting her in the dank, dark dirt,
filling the spaces around her
with his continued absence—
the way he dropped her off,
a bad habit she developed well.
Did he at least gift her crayons, tips broken
or brand-new?

Did he give her canvas so she can draw a world
in hopes of getting it right
next time?

HAPPY HOUR

haiku
It's not often I
have no words to express, but
you leave me speechless.

I fill the glass with ice;
the chilled tequila flows over and around.
I consider shooting it,
think better of it—
not wanting the burn
to overshadow the burn
smoldering behind my eyes.

I will not pour it like libation;
you are not dead,
not lacking heartbeat or pulse.
You are not dead,
standing on your two legs,
eyes seeing everything.

The part that died
inside your mobile corpse
are parts tainted by lies
and misinformation of your own concoction.
I want to write a letter—
open—
in hopes of connecting constellations
you choose to overlook.

I was there,
saw the whole thing,
stitched it to my eyelids
to remember what disbelief tasted like.

I've decided to shoot it,
the tequila resting in ice.
I want the burn now.
If I feel it right,
maybe it will replace your fully-alive death—

performance art turned macabre
turned sitcom.

You are not dead,
but the only way I can watch you
disassemble yourself
is to fill a glass with ice and tequila,
remembering loss isn't something you get over,
but something you get through.

JAI DULANI

MOONLIGHT FIERCE

JAI DULANI IS A QUEER AND TRANS WRITER WHO GREW UP IN PITTSBURGH AND CHANDIGARH, INDIA. HE IS CO-EDITOR OF THE ANTHOLOGY *THE REVOLUTION STARTS AT HOME: CONFRONTING INTIMATE VIOLENCE IN ACTIVIST COMMUNITIES*. **A PUSHCART NOMINATED MULTI-GENRE WRITER, HIS CREATIVE NON-FICTION AND HYBRID WORK HAVE APPEARED IN OR ARE FORTHCOMING IN** *PRAIRIE SCHOONER*, *ALASKA QUARTERLY REVIEW*, *THE OFFING*, **AND ELSEWHERE. HIS POETRY HAS APPEARED PUBLICATIONS SUCH AS** *WAXWING*, *THE RUMPUS*, *NO TOKENS*, **AND** *BEST NEW POETS*. **DULANI HAS RECEIVED FELLOWSHIPS AND RESIDENCIES FROM KUNDIMAN, VONA/VOICES, BLUE MOUNTAIN CENTER, AND THE ASIAN AMERICAN WRITERS' WORKSHOP. HE HOLDS AN MFA IN CREATIVE WRITING FROM WESTERN WASHINGTON UNIVERSITY. DULANI LIVES IN GREENFIELD, MASSACHUSETTS IN A PURPLE HOUSE WITH HIS PARTNER, SON, AND CAT.**

ODE TO BABY DYKE DAYS

black leather butch—you
whisper   we-don't-have-to-do
anything.   sometimes
yes is a revelation.   like
fisting.   arched back
quiver
moan wet.   first taste.

in the tub I lean
back into you   your lips
graze my ear   my knee splashes
hewn flesh   ghosts of blade to thigh

you   reach   touch   say   scar
beautiful.

BED-STUY, 2005.

Black jeans unbuttoned. We are human cartoons.
Mouth inverted. There's nothing like New York
under the moon. That drunken green embrace.
All chest and hand and neck. Too many
vigils. But nothing beats
a Brooklyn house party.
All heat and loose and sweat.
Queers slumber
striped green tactile.
My sister under the coats. Goofy.

Coronas mingle on the IKEA table.
I've had these speakers since high school. Since
my Dad shook his eyes at my teenage want
in the Sony outlet store.
This record is everything.

If you choose the crowd, do you belong?

Naked knife next to table wine. Next
to fresh flowers.
Beside the joint. Behind the fitted.
Stunting.

TATTERED

Icebox night. Officers filmed
our faces. Our breath
in the headlights. Arms locked
blocking Brooklyn bridge.

Uniformed hands ripped
the coffins. Each had a name,
a date of birth / of execution.

They pulled us out of our human
          chain. Arrested us one by one.
Put us in a van. Tightened our cuffs.
Later, we stood in the frigid air,
passed around hand warmers.

          Where are we?
          The cop, she smirked:
                    in the devil's den.

They searched me.
                    male? female?
What are you?

Black tattered cardboard.

Solidarity—
a verb
a howl
a whimper.

SECRET LIVING—

for D.J. Rekha

Breakfast-club-remix—
off-screen-off-script
        Under the staircase temple basement
        Frilly dress drag
playing gin rummy legs out,
drawing cards beyond pawn life.
Beyond American
dream trophies, Black and white.

The king and queen needed us.
We were front row culture war
—Dirty pink origin
        stories. Turquoise trimmed accent
        I was 9, gay kissing Meera at temple summer camp

by the tree—
        Hidden + girl + kiss =A bishop move.

Before her—
        red-headed Christie Mazza
rook tongue on a basement couch.
3rd grade practicing—
        for a future?

In our twenties, diaspora drink in hand—
        we danced Disco Bollywood dance floors.
Brooklyn rooftops. We sang
titillating words of our checkered childhood—

Affirmed our gay
king hair. Our gay
queen outfits. Confessed
our shit management
our checkmate lives.

MY OWN BREATH

in liberation
beyond blood, moonlight fierce.
translate ancestors.

*

Dad was five; saw a
burning Sikh man. Mob thrown oil.
I am a castle.

retro sentimental spawn
pre-1947
civil war civil war civil

*

a half-burned tree.
Ma knit me a very long
sweater once. Ha ha.

I loved it. Gold wool
cables covered my chest.
Sewing runs in the family.

One day I will learn.
The cat keeps digging.
Purple blue lamp on.

*

We're home six days after
miscarriage abortion. Out-
side red leaves ready to fall.

Pitter patter sigh.
Tea mug thumps coffee table.
Wooosh. Cars pass us by.

CENTO[1] FOR US

What is the opposite of devastation? Fruit?
I pin self onto the floor pleasure. How luminous
my non-speech. My nipples
so hard pushing out
the silk of our need
in silence wild. Each river has its source
its course, its life. all my
small actions and inactions
drop away. somewhere
in the night a mouth is singing.
Somebody is always singing —
songs were not allowed. A grass chorus
moves shhhhh through half-propped windows.
i am witnessing her in whatever state
her body will allow. The song moving through
the city like a widow. Our ancient great aunts
and their long slow eyes. You have to face
the underside of everything you've loved.
Each sun sinks itself
in my mouth. Grinding so finely
a stiff bright fate.

---

1 Poems: "The Laceration" by Dawn Lundy Martin; "Recombinant" by Ching-In Chen; "A careful list of all my failures" by Muriel Leung; "We Pretended She Was a Young Boy" by Chrystos; On Wishes by Mahmoud Darwish; A White Poem by Helen Shanley; "I Am Not Ready To Die Yet" by Aracelis Girmay; "100 Bells" by Tarfia Faizullah; from "Steady Summer" by Layli Long Soldier

AT THE THREADING SALON

stretching eyelid skin
    my people shape me.

thread dangling their mouth,
    pain plucked, I hear Hindi,
    laughter. The joke—my gender.

they didn't know I understood
            our language.   Eyes closed
           stillness is not always
consensual.

SOMATICS

This is not something I imagined. I am lifting
weights in my living room. Bending
my knees. Grunting. Plopping

on the couch, between sets.
Hand pushing armrest,
while the other arm rows. Never thought I'd know

what cat cow is. Commodification made me
uninterested. Before that, bewilderment, in general.

I'm used to losing this fight—

—being in my body. Sticking
to what's hard. Muscles

stronger, I am working
on feeling everything
more.

DO YOU LIKE LIVING IN GREENFIELD?

I got Ma'am-ed at the Stop 'N Shop
Actually it's a blur. It was

"you gals." This sexy beard,
useless.

There's a 24 hour CVS down the street
giving: New-York-City-
vibes. It's big-ass lot gives it
away: You're
in a main-street-small-town.

I love me
some brick and stone. One
night I yelled at a dude who was on
something that made him follow me.

I can walk in the woods close
by. Watch my cat eat grass
in the backyard. He loves being

outside. His little head bobbing,
chewing more air
than grass.

ASSIMILATION

16, tentative like unopened mail.
Late 90s Pittsburgh
next to me, Chastity

a blond tank in AP History
chubby face spat

Pocahontas bitch

Wrong Indian, Chastity
(I didn't say)

In gym class, she chucked
a used tampon at me

bloody white girl
(I didn't say)

Chastity's gonna work at a gas station
for the rest of her life big sister comforted me.

Hmmm.
Where are you now Chastity?

I'm ready to meet you on the playground

explode on behalf of every slur.

JACK FRITSCHER

LIVE AGAIN

JACK FRITSCHER, THE FOUNDING EDITOR-IN-CHIEF OF THE SAN FRANCISCO VERSION OF *DRUMMER* **(1977-1980), PRO-ACTIVELY SOLICITED MANY POETS' EROTIC WORK FOR THE MAGAZINE. BORN IN 1939, HE WAS THE BICOASTAL LOVER OF ROBERT MAPPLETHORPE WHOM HE HAS POETIZED OFTEN. HIS OWN FIRST POEM WAS PUBLISHED IN 1957 AND DOZENS OF OTHERS HAVE APPEARED IN** *THE JAMES WHITE REVIEW*, *THE JOSEPHINUM REVIEW*, *THE HOMOSURREALISM JOURNAL*, **AND MANY OTHER MAGAZINES AND POETRY ANTHOLOGIES. HE IS THE WINNER OF THE ORGASMIC POETRY FESTIVAL AWARD (2000) AND THE NATIONAL LEATHER ASSOCIATION'S "LIVING IN LEATHER" POETRY AWARD (2020). HE EARNED HIS DOCTORATE AT LOYOLA UNIVERSITY OF CHICAGO IN 1967 WRITING ABOUT THE POEMS AND PLAYS OF TENNESSEE WILLIAMS. HIS THIRTY BOOKS OF GAY HISTORY AND FICTION, INCLUDING HIS SIGNATURE NOVEL, THE 1990 LAMMY AWARD FINALIST,** *SOME DANCE TO REMEMBER: A MEMOIR-NOVEL OF SAN FRANCISCO 1970-1982*, **ARE POSTED FREE TO ALL READERS AND RESEARCHERS AT WWW.JACKFRITSCHER.COM.**

THE MINESHAFT
835 WASHINGTON STREET
THE MEATPACKING DISTRICT
(FOR UPTON SINCLAIR)

Beautiful it was
in the 800 block of Washington
at Little West 12th
next door to the fumidity of the Mineshaft
the Hudson River a block away
walking past gorgeous sides of fresh red meat
carried after midnight from idling trucks
across the shoulders of strong young Teamsters
a butch ballet in bloody white aprons
carrying slaughter from trucks
engines idling in the dark music of night nosed in
to the fence and weeds and trash
under the elevated freight train tracks
of the crumbling High Line
an army of butchers ignoring leathermen
wearing expensive cow hides
carrying carcasses across cobbles
glistening with dew and blood and fat
lugging the striated red flesh of cows pigs lambs
up under the fluorescent-bright metal awning
over the meatpacking dock
hoisting flesh to hang upside down
a fashion show on meat hooks
revolving on a stainless-steel conveyor
like shirts at a dry cleaner
disappearing the fresh kill to a backroom abbatoir
clamor voices laughter curses

What a gift it was
in those first newly liberated years
to be able to be meat every once and awhile
to play at lambs led to a laughter of slaughter

in a lifetime surrounded by prigs
so moral and ignorant
they judge it is a bad thing:
such enfleshment,
such incarnation of self,
such becoming flesh
that is, well, the very heart
of non-ironic theologies
Saint Pat's on Fifth Avenue
turning bread and wine
into the body and blood of God
the Mineshaft on Washington
turning the body and blood of gay pain
into the soul and divinity of orgasm.

New Age folks brag
flesh sex leads to spirituality.
I'm talking about
flesh sex leading to animality.
After all,
we are equal parts meat and spirit
and I've never minded celebrating body and soul.

In the sanctuary of the Mineshaft,
the word was made flesh.

For a writer inventing new words for
the Love That Once Dare Not Speak Its Name,
what coinage could better?

MAPPLETHORPE

Caro Roberto!
He loved cameras, Kools, Coke, and
for three sine-wave years me
flying round-trips together SFO-JFK
lying in each other's post-coital arms
slugabed on his mattress
on his black plank floor
bonded at 24 Bond Street
his photographer's tongue
licked my writer's eye
in the morning rolling
hard over me
to reach the ringing phone
saying "Ciao, Principessa,"
loving princesses actresses dancers
and the seven-foot calla lilies
in my California garden.

"Patti's a genius," he confided
canonizing her face twin androgyne with his
screening me rushes of Patti in *Moving* and
Robert Having His Nipple Pierced
(Patti keening poems of his masochism
on the soundtrack)
while his kitchen table top caught fire
from his forgotten cigarette.

There were always three people
in his love affairs.
Gone, touring, singing
marrying someone else, widowed,
the Smith girl burned
fuse and muse in his brain.
She was he and he was she
in his solo portraits of her and himself.

At the after-hours Mineshaft bar
the democracy of anonymous sex
leveled the playing field of stardom
for the hunter with a camera
cool, coked, coy,
a voyeur aloof
turning the two floors of wild orgy
into a casting call
turning sex to art.

He ran his career
like a department store
ambushing trendy couples
in SoHo galleries, double-daring,
"If you don't like this picture,
maybe you're not
as avant garde as you think."

He was the goat-footed Pan
a horned satyr
holding my hand in restaurants
shopping together
down Christopher Street
for small Satanic bronzes
invoking
Verlaine
Rimbaud
Baudelaire
inspiring his own
famous flowers of evil
pistils and stamens
vaginas and cocks.

Late one night
I sat in the gunsite of his camera
witnessing him work
his process cool without drama.

"I love you,"
he/I said,
as he shot me, until
three years of lust
evaporated to sweet friendship.

At the end, dying young,
he filmed flowers more than faces
because he could no longer
stand eyes looking back at him
through the safety glass of his lens.

He loved. She loved. I loved.
To me, his seed. To her, his ashes.

MAPPLETHORPE AND ME

A NEW YORK LOVE AFFAIR
(A SHOOTING SCRIPT)

INTERIOR. MANHATTAN PLAYROOM - NIGHT - MEDIUM SHOT

2 men naked kneeling kneecap to kneecap.
Gunfighter gun play from gay bar saloons.
Hit men packing heat. Gun oil greasing torsos.
Erect. Loaded. Silencers. Mute.
Beyond words better left unsaid.

A and B who is A who is B
stroking a brace of pistols trading handguns
unholstered cock
amygdala algorithms
of gun lust/fear/anxiety/sadness.
Grunt/grin/spit/tongue/lick weapons,
rimming the bore
the ammo of *amor*
hazarding risky roulette
in a perilous plague,
a season in hell,
playing under
the "Gun Blast" silver-gelatin photo
gun-crazy Mapplethorpe
shot for Rimbaud
shot by Verlaine
with a 7mm six-shooter
loaded with
opium and absinthe.

CAMERA TRACKS IN VERY SLOWLY TO CAPTURE ACTION IN ONE CONTINUOUS SHOT

as slow as the 2 marksmen, touching chests,
scratch pistol muzzles nipple to nipple
each clocked in the other's gun site, bulls-eye,
locking arms, groom & groom intertwining
strong wrists/biceps/firearms to drink
the champagne of their blood wedding,
Saturday night special
duel in the dark
gunslingers, pistol-whip blood lust
groans, huffs of panting breath
snuffing out a candle with a bullet
eyes wide dilated
lightning-fast slow-motion quick draw
taking aim, hands gripping gunstock butts
hardon of cold steel barrels
parting equal each other's lips.

CAMERA PUSH-IN 2-SHOT CLOSE-UP

Parting the beloved's bared teeth
no one but him puts a pistol in his mouth
taking aim, both stare down the barrels of true love
in the other's gun hand
into the other's squinting eyes
biting down, sucking the cold metal taste of the barrel
tasting like graphite and olives
brokeback gambling men,
trigger fingers on hair triggers,
fists on rampant cocks cocked,
eyeball to eyeball, cocked,
countdown, on three, cocked,
crack shots, cum bullets, adrenalin rush,
leaving tea and cakes and civilization behind.

Click-Click-Click
of the spinning pistol chambers
empty, unloaded under the animal roar
the thrill-kill draining of anxiety
shooting their loads up belly and chest
into the target hearts.

CAMERA MEDIUM SHOT HOLDS ON

Two men in *La petite mort* collapse.

CUE MUSIC UP

"Bang! Bang! My Baby Shot Me Down!"

SUPERIMPOSE TITLE

Never let's become ordinary to each other.
Sex. Death. Art.

THE END

Roll credits over Mapplethorpe photo
"Gun Blast" 1985.

MOONLIGHT SERENADE

SUMMER 1939
(FOR THE 50TH ANNIVERSARY OF STONEWALL)

1

Quick queers in the Sixties and Seventies
born in the Depression Thirties
and the boomer Forties
Radio music and 78-rpm records
the soundtrack to the world war
of our detonating childhoods
grown men marching away
leaving us pierced to the heart
crying in pre-school panic
re-curled into fetal thumb sucking
curdling into romantic yearning,
morose delectation for them.

2

Surviving silent
the conformity of the Fifties,
Jimmy Dean on the Drive-In screen,
rock and roll spinning teen angels
centrifuge toward rebellion with cause,
unbeaten beatniks beating bongos
caffeinated coffee house howling
waking us to our twenties
outspoken in the Sixties and Seventies,
we war babies
politics personal
flowers in our hair
striking campuses
constructing resistance
protesting war
marching for civil rights

driving Old Dixie down
finding strength by facing fear
raging into Stonewall.

3

A hundred movies nostalgic
for war and remembrance
begin on screen
"Summer 1939"
the last anxious summer
before war book-ended love stories,
birthing my queer story:
during the bright noon hour
of that year's longest day,
Midsummer's Eve,
born of my sire, born of my dam,
Summer Solstice
sacramental sex magic
pulsing holy rhythms in my brain.

In movie palaces, incoming
through the window of the screen,
newsreel atrocities
in a world gone mad
unreeling in black and white
between a musical and a western
corpses of children hanging by their thumbs
shocking our innocence with trauma,
hardening fear of death
into death-defying eros,
reaching the age of reason
and anxiety at six,
battle-weary little men
refusing to play soldier
knowing too much too soon
when the war, which wars never do, ended

and the men came marching home again
hoorah hoorah
in their gabardine uniforms
smelling of barracks and cigarettes and aftershave
tossing us kids up High Joy into the air
catching us in their strong arms
because we were what they were fighting for
until we had to fight them,
those veterans suddenly seeing who we are.

4

I will die wanting to forget
ration stamps for food, for coffee,
for shoes, for nylons, for typewriters,
no gas, no tires, no cars,
nightly blackouts
air-raid wardens patrolling
our dark neighborhood sidewalks,
lights out in every house,
as we sat sweet lilac night
visiting on summer porches,
a parley of women and boys and girls,
talking of peas in our victory gardens
rocking on wooden chairs,
the metal porch gliders gone for scrap
for armored tanks and battle ships,
talking of soldiers
husbands fathers brothers sons gone,
tolerating kindly the porch-step company
of one inconvenient young man 4F
with flat feet and glasses and violet eyes,
a lodger sharing his ration book for a spare room,
so bashful a bachelor, so book in hand, so nice
and down the block in the tender June night
we could hear a lonely woman,
mannish, they called her,

playing “Moonlight Serenade”
on her Victrola,
humming a love song
to her bob-cropped darling
serving far away,
a quarter century before,
woke with war,
our marginal militia
of Marsha and Sylvia
cast the first Stonewall stone.

DANCING TO REMEMBER

Some afternoons
their rooftop security cameras
recorded him
slow-dancing his nude Tai Chi
to music in the secluded garden
they planted as an outdoor library
Walt Whitman lilacs
Robert Frost birches
Marlene Dietrich linden
Mapplethorpe calla lilies
Faulkner roses for Emily
sleeping with the gay dead.

He moved stretched breathed
to become one with the bodies and spirits
of thousands of nude gay men of every look
one-spirited, two-spirited, trans-spirited,
spirited away, too soon, too soon,
dancing the divine melancholy
of Satie's *Gymnopédies*.

He remembered his friends
disappearing from
surging streets
juke-box bars
jam-packed discos
restaurants
with empty chairs and empty tables
twice as many dead from plague
than died in Vietnam
remembered them all
those sexy men,
each and all sexy in their way
who came from everywhere
living it up when

Beautiful People
of all kinds of strange beauty,
even the hot off-beat ones
who looked like Picasso experimented,
cruised the Titanic 1970s
before the iceberg of AIDS.

Beauty was their vocation.
Some of them,
some of his Folsom Street tricks,
like the horse-hung young hippie stallion
in the orgy room at the Barracks bath
whose thick blond braids
he pulled back like reins
came so hot to his memory
they materialized
like glowing outlines
of wire figures
written in thin air
by kids waving
burning sparklers in the dark
like Cocteau's
luminous lighting paintings
like Beatrice Lillie's
fairies dancing
at the bottom of their garden.

FOR FEDERICO GARCIA LORCA
(1898-1936)
MURDERED BY FASCISTS

I am a flower
and my hand is my sun
that warms to life
the flower in me.
Lorca they say was
killed by Falangist bandits
with a shot up the ass for being queer.
He died
like I die
in a fertile country.

But I live again
after each petite death
of supreme forgetting:
the aloneness the dark root
of a scream.
I must make
the protein flower grow
to crush down inside me
the shriek that stands on tiptoe
waiting to remind me
that I am no one else.

I build my purl-veined harrow
of astonished flesh,
I cultivate the blood flower
of forgetting.

But my sun melts my harrow,
melts the paraffin flower
that blanches,
runs like liquid camellia,
dissolving to forgetting,

for getting the fore-gotten
sentence of aloneness.

And I wonder
what were Falangist bandits
and if they did any good
in the garden of bitter rosebay

FOR ANDY WARHOL, NICO, AND THE VELVET UNDERGROUND

(THE EXPLODING PLASTIC INEVITABLE TOUR 1966)

Chains on shiny
shiny boots of leather
musk of black jackets
hung in a row

Come on Monday
Wednesday Thursday
Come on Friday
See the show

Crack of whip
iron-studded leather
drip of wax on
sweating skin

Outside the door-bolt
rev of motor cycles
Iron Crosses
Come see the show

Stretched like Jesus
by shiny boots of leather
God will get you
if you don't watch out

A HUSBAND DRIVES INTO A CLARK GAS STATION MICHIGAN 1969

Summer-parents, young, worn,
driving aimless past dusk
circling through town
to cool off, cool down,
with wagon windows
overflowing with two wild tots,
green through the glass
in the buggy fluorescence
of this small filling station,
soft with light,
where I work late shifts alone,
inviting in the night
to a crowded husband
with a dollar bill
who stalls for time
for two and a half gallons
at 39.9 cents
to avoid going home
with his gum-popping wife
and his two green brats
already pajamaed,
sweaty, sticky with candy,
whining for Coca-Cola.

In his side-view mirror
he watches me,
hot, cool, twenty-six,
and embarrassed for him
embarrassed for himself.
I crouch down to fill his tank.
"Take your time, bud," he calls back,

elbow out his window,
winking in the mirror
the pregnant wife cannot see,
nodding,
taking his moment with me.

I cap his tank
and take his dollar,
his fingers touch mine,
eyes saving me up for later,
his grin, my grin, launching him
with his wife and fluorescent green kids
off into the darkness that is his alone,
with his hunting dog tied to a tree
out front of his house
with two cups
unwashed
in her kitchen sink.

THE YOUNG TURKS DREAM OF DEREK JARMAN

The beautiful young migrants
trafficked in Sardinia
sweating in steel mills
hanged by the wrists
strung up for whipping
Young men naked,
greasy, hairy, filthy slaves,
beaten by the foreman,
the whipmaster, hanging
the bound young men
upside-down
suspended stripped
naked for punishment.

The leather whip cuts across
young muscled backs.
Somebody's sons.
Somebody's brothers.
One, a great beauty,
a Caghineri convicted
of crimes against nature,
suspended by his spread ankles.
The handsome slave,
more perverse than the whipmaster,
grows hard,
beaten by the muscular foreman.

They know not they are watched
close-up and from a distance online
by men who enjoy
brutally sensuous punishment.

Young men born to suffer
working at hard labor
trapped in a Sardinian migrant prison
sentences indeterminate
pulled from solitary confinement
to labor by the sweat of greasy muscle.

Hard
they are, one by one,
stretched spreadeagle
suspended upside-down
by their boots
spread against steel grills
bound tied whipped
in the male sensuality
of young men serving time
serving a cruel master
punished
in the nightmare
of a dream gone bad
in a steel dungeon.

OLD SOULS LAST NIGHT ON YOUTUBE IN 1903

Last night on YouTube
in "The Oldest Ever Photos of England,"
I paused the high-definition colorized video
when I spied you on screen
in your home-spun work clothes
ragged shirt and vest open down your throat
your first mustache drooping sad
on your resolute young face
seventeen orphaned for six years
standing in stopped time
120-some years ago in 1903
in a crowd of destitute working men
and desperate boys
Victorian rag-pickers and mudlarks
standing quiet hungry outside
a Salvation Army Barracks in London
during the morning crush
of yawning men having waked
in beds twopence a night
in lodging houses
finding a charity meal ticket
dropped by Salvationists
on their bunks during the night
queuing up for a farthing breakfast
a quarter of a penny
cheese and crust
with Jesus Christ.
I wanted to travel back in time
like the movies and save you.

ALEX GILDZEN

POINT THE WAY

ALEX GILDZEN IS A TRUE ELDER OF OUR COMMUNITY: A POET, ARTIST, AND CULTURAL WITNESS WHO DANCED AT STONEWALL, SMOKED POT WITH ALLEN GINSBERG, AND WAS DRAWN BY DAVID HOCKNEY. HIS POETRY DEBUTED IN *KENT QUARTERLY* **IN 1962, HIS FIRST CHAPBOOK FOLLOWED IN 1969, AND SINCE THEN HIS WORK HAS SPANNED PRINT, PERFORMANCE, AND PROTEST. HE HAS STOOD AT THE HEART OF GAY AND QUEER ART FOR MORE THAN HALF A CENTURY. HIS BOOK,** *A LITTER OF LISTS*, **IS FORTHCOMING FROM SIBLING RIVALRY PRESS. INSTAGRAM @GILDZEN**

WHAT WAS IT LIKE THE YOUNG ASK

my memory of dancing
at Stonewall before the riot
has begun to fade
but on another nite
I sat alone at Julius
drinking & cruising
& I saw thru the window a vision
a princess with tiara
& full length white gloves
skated past waving a wand
it was Rollerena
making history with each wave
& it still is Rollerena
skating thru the decades
who I see & always will
& I will tell the young
deciding which way to go
to look for her to tap
their shoulders with her wand
then point the way

BREAKFAST WITH BOB

you died
before I cd give you
this Lucy mug
so I sit here
sipping coffee from it
& eating pancakes
on which I tried
to write a poem

3 weeks ago
I wd've written you
abt that failure
setting you up
for a smart ass reply
that of course
the vanilla I used as ink
wd disappear
into a pancake's flesh

I take another sip
& put down the mug
Lucy looks at me
tells me you know
tells me it's all right
to write on pancakes

RICHARD HOWARD CALLD ME A COCKTEASE

I think it was Coby Britton
who told me that

was it before or after the time
I visitd his farm
the time his partner came to my bed
& sd "Coby wants the 3 of us to sleep together"
I declind

I remember once thinking
I shd write memoirs
calld The Boy Who Sd No

I cd recount Ginsberg
pounding on my door
shouting "Alex....   Alex...."
& me on the other side
remaining silent

but then there were enuf yeses
to fill an even bigger book
one I'll never write

we get old
& liaisons dissipate
the dead keep no ledger
when it gets cold at nite
I wrap myself in the arms
of all those men
who for however long
loved me as deeply
as I loved them
their embraces tease me
to sleep

DOWLING'S LAST PERSIMMON

in memory of
Stephen Sondheim

my teeth sink into
flesh of the divine fruit
I savor the taste
knowing this is the final one
from an old orchard
soon to be rippd out
to make room
for an industrial warehouse

& when I'm done
I carefully put the calyx
into an envelope
so that whoever finds it
mite turn an ending
into a beginning

PLAYING AROUND

by the pool
I see a young man
in a speedo
so shiney
I want to run
my hand over it

over those hillocks
& that bump
in the road

but he doesn't see me

so I walk back
to the patio
to my pen & paper
where words become hands
& I can play
for as long as I want

CHAD'S FEET

after the dance
the blood
the bruise

there is a cost
for beauty

the dancer knows
yet still throws himself
into the air

there
he & we meet
in the act of art

WHILE READING POEMS BY MARK WITH TITLES BY TOM

"I want to sing jingles…"
stops me cold

I gulp coffee
& look straight ahead

I see Don Javor
for the first time

walking down the hallway
on the 12th floor of the library

his jeans loose enuf
to allow his cock to sway

he's like Lana Turner
in "They Won't Forget"

that quick promenade
that sticks in yr head forever

VALENTINE'S DAY

neither chocolate
nor a naked man
came to my door

but a new friend
told me
when she sd my name
to an old friend
silent with dementia
he broke into song

love
doesn't need
a red bow
to be love

COGITATING

that's what I call it
when I retreat
to the patio
to get away
from the world
that wants me

robocall from Turkey
spam from Russia
mailbox full of ads
for hearing-aides
& burial services

sitting on a metal chair
I stare at mountains
sometimes walk
to near twin palms
& lean against them
creating stanzas
in my head

I'm never alone
with this world
outside my door

sometimes I sit
til the sun goes
behind the mountains

I remember
the old woman
at the pastry shop
in Buenos Aires
& the dancer
with the video camera
in West Hollywood

I plot where to gift
what I believe are my treasures

my mind creates
a czardas of verbs

I cogitate
then go inside
to dice garlic
for my salad

NOT QUITE A LOVER

that's what I calld
my Southern beau
from years ago

the men from then
never really leave
even when they die

but I ache
to taste his salt
one last time

instead a tear must do
& a smile
that says "thank you"

MICKIE KENNEDY
ENOUGH TO KNOW

MICKIE KENNEDY IS A LATE-BLOOMING GAY, NOT UNLIKE AN EARLY-DYING MOTH: LIGHT-DRUNK, LOTS OF F(L)APPING. HIS FIRST CHAPBOOK, *GLANDSCAPES*, WON THE 2025 BUTTON POETRY CHAPBOOK CONTEST. HIS FIRST BOOK OF POETRY, *WORTH BURNING*, WILL BE PUBLISHED BY BLACK LAWRENCE PRESS IN FEBRUARY 2026. HE AND HIS PARTNER RANDY SPLIT THEIR TIME BETWEEN BALTIMORE COUNTY AND REHOBOTH BEACH, AND THEY ARE CURRENTLY LOCKED IN A LONG-STANDING COMPETITION TO SEE WHO CAN BE BLOCKED ON GRINDR THE MOST.
WWW.MICKIEKENNEDY.COM
INSTAGRAM: @MICKIEPOET

PROSTATE HIEROPHANY

The plastic wand is slightly thicker
than my husband's finger, and topped
with a bulbous head. Inside, twelve needles
nestled like wasp stingers. I'm lying

fetal in a paper gown, my ass on display
for a doctor who's coating the wand
with K-Y Jelly, the brand they use
in pornos. He slides the device

so easily inside me. *I'm experienced,*
I say, but he's not in the mood
for humor. An industrial thunk. The first
needle collects a hair-thin jab

of tissue. I thought it would hurt
far more than it does.
Each pulse so quick and loud I lose
the pain. When he's taken what he needs,

the doctor swabs me with a wet wipe.
Cautious, tender, like a mother
during toilet training. *Don't look at it*—
and I don't, but that doesn't stop

the sound: a fleshy slap
when it hits the biohazard bin.
Later that night, I ask my husband
to jack me off. He looks surprised,

but knows better than to argue with a maybe
dying man. He touches me
like he's afraid of catching my mortality—
quick, furtive. When I cum, he runs

for a towel. The doctor told me this
could happen, but how do you prepare
for a miracle—water into wine,
semen into blood.

DEAREST PROSTATE

Today, your first crush
of radiation. A three-way—
you, me, and the young technician
with an Amish beard,
his hands far softer than my husband's.

It's Valentine's Day. The irony
is almost worth the loss.
So soon you'll be a lump
of scar tissue, walnut-sized, a death
for my little death machine.

The massager in my nightstand,
gnarled as my mother's knuckles,
useless now. Randy's fingers,
trained to find you without eyes,
forever caressing an absence.

Still, we will always have Miami,
the daddy with the boomerang curve
and the brass bull ring.
And we'll always have the first time
we met, the end

of a hairbrush, slickened
with olive oil. My dear, my dear,
I had to choose myself.
But without you, my tender
tumescence, I'll become a non-

practicing gay, like my uncle,
who flayed his heart and froze the meat.
A peeling flamingo guards his yard,
a final scrap of flair
from a long-gone lover. So much

long-gone, but he still has you.
His version of you.
And so do I—my knot
of nothingness. My withered radish.
Not gone, just dead.

BREACH: A PLAY IN THREE PARTS

Act I, Scene I

Tommy's left hand submerged
in a bucket thick with ice.
A neat, sunlit kitchen.
Minutes pass. He wants
to be numb enough.
With a scalpel he stole
from his father's office,
he shears flat warts
from his fingers. He wants
to be beautiful. Blood
fills the tiny craters.

Act I, Scene II

Tommy and Mickie alone in a walk-up attic.
It looks like they're stepping on eyes,
the floorboards made from knotted pine.
Tommy opens a tin and pours
liquid mercury into the bowl of his hands.
The metal jitters like a body.
The wing of an owl sputters from a rafter.

Act I, Scene III

A scatter of car magazines.
A mattress on the floor.
Slightly damp dollar bills
tossed on the sheets. Tommy leans
against the wall. He's dressed
in his mother's satin lingerie,
brassiere sagging with water balloons
he filled with a garden hose.
Mickie stands a foot away, afraid
he'll touch the wrong thing.

Act II, Scene I

Tommy and Mickie alone on a loveseat,
close but not quite touching.
An exposed bulb in a frat basement,
a swaying pull-chain.
In Tommy's lap: a ball point pen,
a strip of aluminum foil, a stolen
lighter, and a plastic bottle—a hole
cored through the cap.
Tommy unzips a tiny Ziploc,
and Mickie pretends it's full
of salt, snow, teeth.

Act II, Scene II

Before a housefly settles
on a half-eaten bagel, it visits
a mug, a lamp, a window, a lip.

Act II, Scene III

[A landline screams]

Who is this?
[Silence]
Tommy, is that you? Do you need help?
[Silence]
Are you there?
[Silence]

[A landline screams]

Act III Scene I

An email:

Mickie, car broke down in Tennessee
mountains. Engine went to shit. Mom
in hospital. Lymphoma. It's bad. Need
cash so I can see her. I hate
asking, but you know me.
I'm your Tommy.
Western Union Food City #611.
Pay to: my name.

Act III Scene II

Neon shoving through drawn shades.
The crush of gravel in a motel lot.
Above the bed, off-kilter, a framed giraffe
folding itself in half to drink.
A woman guides Tommy's hand
to her bra strap. She's dressed
in lace, sunspots on her breasts.
The money is gone. The drugs, gone.
She takes his cock inside her mouth.
Tommy mortars shut his eyes.

Act III Scene III

A manicured backyard garden.
Mickie teeters at the top of a ladder,
his body wearing an oak
like a condom. His wife
strokes across the pool.
Slowly, calmly, he slides the tip
of his finger inside
a vespid wasp's paper nest.

FAUX HOMO

The first time Randy sashayed a bootleg Birken
in public, I thought I was prepared
for it, thought I was ready for the men

in lifted trucks who might take bats
to both our heads, because I'd taken
small but real steps towards Randy's brand

of freedom—a red sequin jacket
I've never worn, a Dolly Parton bobblehead
gyrating on my dash.

Randy wanted to hold my hand,
but I couldn't give myself that softness.
Not in the South. Not on the lip of a busy street,

wide-hipped Suburbans rumbling past.
Of course it happened—a bald man hurled
faggots from his half-rolled window.

It smacked like a baseball into a mitt. It smacked
like my mother's fist. I stood there,
more mannequin than man,

while Randy shot his middle finger in the air.
Goddam purse. I wanted to shove it
deep inside a woodchipper. I wanted to gut it

like a big-mouth bass. I wanted Randy
to be what he's not—ashamed,
like me.

NO HOMO

In his bedroom
after school I touched
his dick. I wanted
to kiss him, but he said
kissing was too gay.
He made the rules,
I obeyed. *I'm not*
a fag, he said, *just horny.*
Sweat from his face
fell on my chest.
He stooped and kissed
a drop, then my lips.
I'm only kissing you, he said,
because you want it.

SEX EDUCATION

Smothered sounds pulled me down
the stairs. I caught my mother
on the living room floor
with Charlie, her new boyfriend.
He was hairy everywhere
except his head, which was smooth
as a roll-on deodorant stick.
I was young, but old enough to know
what they were doing—strewn
clothes, the floral rug
pockmarked with cans. Burning
with their bodies, I crept
inside my room. Before Charlie,
me. Before me, my father.
Before my father, my mother alone
in the tobacco fields,
mashing caterpillars for pennies.
That night, she wouldn't
slur her way beneath my sheets,
but it felt like she was there, watching me
slide the lock and lower my briefs.

HARDENING

Randy teases my nipple with his teeth. He's careful,
filling me with not quite pain. An idea

of pain. These days, radiated twice a week,
almost nothing gets me hard—my cock a vole

hiding in the grass. One scene still works,
or almost works, injecting me with an approximation

of desire: white gloves in a dark room, stainless steel,
and a needle—slow, certain—sewing shut

my mother's bloodless lips. And there it is,
a downstairs twitch. *It's alive*, Randy says, gripping

as I stiffen. He thinks I'm thick with his touch,
not the grit of her imagined end. A recluse

riffling through tubs of DVDs, her mind
gone patchy as a water-damaged wall. She's far

too feeble to hurt me like she used to, defanged
by time. But O, the thought of her

pallid hands. The thought of her powdered
face, the loamy plot, the dirt's wet scratch

against the coffin's glossy lid—God,
the blood roars in.

PROGRAMMED CELL DEATH

A velvety lounge. He flashed
his cock at the urinal trough, took me
home. I was new to that game, afraid

of my insides. Without any bones,
an octopus can wrench itself
through tiny holes—a quarter-sized gap

in glass, an open mouth. He flipped me
face down, the rasp of his beard
becoming the tap of a cock.

The octopus has an almost human
intelligence—solving puzzles,
taking things apart. *Relax*, he said,

pushing. When the male inserts
his hectocotylus, he keeps the rest
of his body far away, terrified

his mate will confuse him for a meal.
I asked him to stop. He listened,
sort of. He didn't shove

beyond the tip, but he didn't
pull out. Alone in his bed,
I heard the metallic clang

of a beer tab hitting the counter,
the flare of late-night news.
I felt lucky. After copulation,

the octopus begins to die, betrayed
by its own body—all three hearts
dismantled from the inside out.

BUSH RIVER BOOKS AND VIDEO

The glory holes, hidden within
the muskiest corners, are always swarming

with married men, their wedding rings
catching the blacklight. Inside the het room,
straight porn on a giant plasma for straight men

with spines more erect than their cocks.
They're gay enough to let the gays go down.

The homo room—crusted shag, hideous
velvet—never more than half full.
Me and Randy wander aimlessly,

our pockets bulging with paper towels.
The first time, unprepared, we drove home

with damp boxers. He leads me
to a loveseat, his hand a leash
on the back of my neck. Maybe ten of us,

jittery with nerves, scattered far apart.
On the screen, a twink slushes

a pumpkin with his monstrous cock.
His groans ooze wetly from the speakers.
Nobody knows how to start, or what's too far,

until an older man against the wall unbuttons
his jeans, flopping free, and suddenly

everyone is undoing themselves.
The metal babble of belt buckles. Zippers
fumbled open. And almost instantly,

kneeling before us, a hovering mouth
attached to a face more shadow than flesh.

Randy's cock, the cock I love, disappears
inside the shadow's mouth. He tosses his head,
lost. The screen-twink jacks himself

with pulp. I watch it happen, all of it, hard
as I've ever been. Hard because I'm not

involved. It doesn't last long—
a gasp, and the mouth becomes a man
slipping back to where he was. We crawl

inside our pants. Ourselves again.

VIVA VIAGRA!

I have a terrible case of penis scurvy.
The cure—drill a hole in an orange
and make love to the orange.
I can't make love to the orange. So soft,
I'd struggle to pleasure

a month-old mango. My husband calls
my cock the Bubonic Dick. What happened
to oceans of wind-swept spunk?
To boners as endless as waves? To hard
as a hull, wet as a shoal? These days,

each time I arrive, I feel
that final edge: when jizz becomes jazz;
when ass becomes ash;
when cum becomes came.

DRIEN THOMPSON
KISS-SWOLLEN

DRIEN THOMPSON GREW UP BELIEVING BLACK PEOPLE WERE THE MAJORITY—SURROUNDED BY STRONG-WILLED BLACK FAMILIES AND INDIVIDUALS WHO SHAPED THEIR EARLY WORLD. THEIR MOVE TO A PREDOMINANTLY WHITE TOWN BEFORE HIGH SCHOOL FORCED A REDEFINITION OF IDENTITY, AND ART BECAME THE SPACE WHERE THEY COULD PRESERVE THEMSELF, HEAL, AND ARTICULATE WHO THEY WERE BECOMING. THOMPSON EARNED A BA IN ART WITH MINORS IN HONORS INTERDISCIPLINARY STUDIES AND MANDARIN CHINESE FROM THE UNIVERSITY OF CENTRAL ARKANSAS IN 2019, WHERE THEY WERE BOTH AN HONORS STUDENT AND PERFORMANCE SCHOLAR. THEIR UNDERGRADUATE THESIS, *THE IMPACT OF AFRICAN ART AND AESTHETICS ON THE WESTERN WORLD*, **EXAMINED WESTERN RESPONSES TO AFRICAN ART FROM THE LATE 1800S THROUGH THE OBAMA ERA. A FREELANCE AND COMMISSIONED ARTIST AND WRITER, THOMPSON FOCUSES ON EXPRESSIVE, INCLUSIVE DEPICTIONS OF THE HUMAN FORM, EMPHASIZING EMOTION OVER IDEAL AND GRANTING ALL COLORS AND BODIES EQUAL ATTENTION. AS AN AFRICAN AMERICAN PERSON OFTEN DENIED THE OPPORTUNITY TO DEFINE THEMSELF, THEY ALLOW THEIR WORK TO SPEAK WITHOUT EXPLANATION—INVITING VIEWERS TO CONFRONT THEIR ASSUMPTIONS AND MEET THE ART ON ITS OWN TERMS.**

PAIRINGS

Stone & Pebble.
Smoke & Fire.
Thunder & Lightning.

Are you best friends,
                                        or are you lovers?
Is there even a difference
                                        (is there even a need)?
Would it matter if my eyes are blind to discernment?

To pair with another,
there must be a connection—
like Bluetooth,
like synced up,
like plugged in.
                                        (I apologize for that last line)

Must have been possessed by
Ghost & Spirit,
Bone & Muscle,
Poltergeist & Demon,
Ankle & Heel.

When I speak of pairings,
I talk not of opposites.
See, orange and blue
may look different
when next to each other,
but they remain the same,
amplified only
by illusions of the eye.

You can look for only so long
before your eyes hurt,
and when they are mixed,
they make mud.

When I talk of complements,

I speak of things that stand
just as worthy
on both sides
of the equal sign =

things that create
delicious mouthfuls
alone and when paired,

things that hold
the limelight in solo
as well as in salsa,

things that double autonomy
rather than halve it.

Finger & Toe.
Nail & Screw.
Paper & Canvas.
As with the partnership
of Me & You.

WITH LEGS

Folded and pressed
into the perfect shape for your pleasure,
positioned to feel every moment.
No way to distraction.
There are several ways to hold my attention, but you do it with
the force to tear my soul from its hinges,
my legs from their sleeve,
my words from their mouth,
my thoughts from their head,
my secrets from their chest.
I've never been one to let loose or be wild,
but when you are around,
my hair is constantly down,
shirt always untucked,
tie perpetually off,
belt consistently unbuckled,
hair lovingly messed,

lips kiss-swollen,

face quite flushed with excitement.

You know, I never end a poem coolly,
but this one deserves aftercare.
It deserves tiny kisses and light touches,
deserves loving caresses and sleepy smiles,
and hugs, and slow-rising chests, and kind eyes,
warm hands and tangled legs,
and sweat and laughter.
How wonderful.

I am grateful that aftercare comes after every poem with you.

A manifestation, a revelation.

There is something brewing inside me.
I ~~think~~ hope it's you.

WHY DID YOU GET THIS NEW SKETCHBOOK?

~~I bought this sketchbook for you.~~
I mean, ~~I bought this sketchbook with you.~~
I mean, I bought this sketchbook…

Fellas, is it gay to fall asleep kissing?
…
To dream with lips touching?
…
Connected homie style?

I bought this sketchbook, ~~so I could post drawings for you to see.~~
I mean, I bought this sketchbook, ~~so I could have another sketchbook to show you when we hung out again.~~
I mean, I bought this sketchbook to get back i
into my creative practice.

Fellas, it is gay to fuck the homie?
I mean, fuck with the homie?
Uh, fuck with the homie heavy?

Fuck
I mean…

I bought this sketchbook, so I could draw you.
~~I mean,~~ I bought this sketchbook so I could draw
you closer to me.
Entice you with talent to distract from my long stares.
~~I mean,~~ I bought this sketchbook so I could memorize your form.
Not just with my eyes and hands, but
with pen, with paint, with paper and pencil.

Take notes so I could be allowed your body's examination,
a ticket to your deepest parts.

I bought this sketchbook to pour out
every vibration my body conjures for you.
Play the record for my mind ad nauseam

Is my answer ~~satisfying~~ cool and mysterious yet?

TRINE

Spoken word grew through three seasons of this strange year.
Winter, spring, and summer with no fall in sight.

(Winter)

In close quarters and smokey haze, a nervous chill tries to hide,
but quiet falls like snow. Laughter freezes into rain.
I would give (or take) anything to stay inside that metal shelter
a moment longer with you.

(Spring)

Silence is usually the rule, yet tonight my anxiety relaxes
and talk becomes joy. Nervousness blooms into possibility,
petals chosen and placed.
A small longing opens for the chance
to hold and be held.

(Summer)

Proximity becomes nearness in space, time, and relationship.
Heat rises in my chest and face, the only science
that explains this shift between us.
We rush into water seeking coolness,
but
          heat rises.

                    There will always be four seasons.
                    Even if you taste nothing sweet,
                    even if your heart stays cold
                    despite every effort, every gift.

Autumn arrives anyway.
One leaf, one breeze, one quiet knock,
is enough to mark its coming.

MUSIC CAN SOUND LIKE THAT

a beep
a jingle
a sound

As if giggling, the heart quivers.
My lungs remind me to breathe.
I've held the oxygen in my hands too tightly.

A word, an image, a sentence if I've been good.

I stare into the black box, like a cat hunting a fly.

Still nothing.

Perhaps I'm more like the feline when chasing a red dot.
Never winning, so excited.
With energy and agitation. I become neurotic
Running for that last satisfactory pounce.

a violent end
a curious glance
a weighty disappointment

I laugh at my own misery to feel community.

a desperate search
a bored face
a passing car

I wrote a sadder poem than intended.

a small conversation
a tinier laugh
a silent sigh

IS IT EVER OKAY TO WANT YOU?

Perspiration beads up on my brow.
A drop falls from my nose
and agitates your lip.
I hope you are unbothered,
distracted by bliss.

Dilated eyes, heightened sense of self.

My back aches, legs tremble,
heart begs to stop,
yet you are relentless,
and I am deaf to the plea.
We start up once more.

How many times will you drink
from the foundation of my body,
stealing my very essence?
Never quite done,
I drain you of yours.

A continuous pounding
of the hips and heart.

Can you hear the cracking
of your own soul?
It renews itself, flexible yet strong.

I felt a hair or two
on short, grateful legs,
contrasted with the ego of my thighs.
I arrogantly tried to take in
all that you are,
my mouth much too small
to even take hold
of the flesh of your neck.

I think longing is a virtue.

LISTEN AGAIN

A soft whisper walks out,

"Where would you like me?"

In my nervousness and haste,
I suddenly realize that I am
trusted
I do not have control, nor
manipulation.

I am given faith,
trust that I would not throw around their vulnerability
or pick off the soul.
Only an expectation of the warmth
that holding begins.
The question, no longer what I hear

"Where would you like to meet me?"

TIGHT THIGHS/LOOSE SKIN

Brown and wide
Thick and tight
No wrap because I am not a present
Your presence is the gift I asked for

I don't want to be a gift. I want to be free.

I love the feeling of your soft skin
You wish a range and movement
That is not yet delivered, unneeded

What if you were flexible enough to
understand my discomfort?

But I only want you
In all forms you take
I want to see, to feel your evolution
Naturally selected to live in my mind

Class and Kingdoms apart.

Tight thighs, please walk by

I must rest.

I WILL FUCK YOU

I'll sing in your ear as I send thunder and lightning coursing through your deepest parts.

I'll cook you a meal so you are familiar with having your mouth filled.

I will drink from your foundation, gulp down the nectar and be thirsty for more.

I will make you remember every thrust I gave to you.

I will fuck you.

I'll have you as my meal in your living room,
your couch my bib,
your moans my music.

I will stand over your kneeling form
and drown you in my flood.

I will devour you.

I will read you to sleep and wake you with my kisses.

I will fuck you.

I will hold your hand and force your mouth wide so you may taste my pleasure, receive me, know me.

I will eat you alive.

I will stare you down as you
vibrate and shake and scream for me.

I will fuck you.

DAVID TRINIDAD
MY SECRET LIFE

DAVID TRINIDAD'S WORK INVESTIGATES THE CULTURAL LANDSCAPES OF AMERICA'S GREAT METROPOLISES, AS WELL AS THE CULTURE AT LARGE. HIS POEMS ARE OFTEN FILLED WITH REFERENCES TO TELEVISION, MOVIES, AND MUSIC, WHILE ALSO BEING POPULATED BY VERY REAL PEOPLE AND PROBLEMS. HIS MOST RECENT BOOKS ARE *NEW PLAYLIST* AND *HOLLYWOOD CEMETERY*. HE IS ALSO THE EDITOR OF *A FAST LIFE: THE COLLECTED POEMS OF TIM DLUGOS*, *PUNK ROCK IS COOL FOR THE END OF THE WORLD: POEMS AND NOTEBOOKS OF ED SMITH*, **AND** *DIVINING POETS: DICKINSON*, **AN EMILY DICKINSON TAROT DECK. HIS WORK HAS APPEARED IN NUMEROUS PERIODICALS AND ANTHOLOGIES, INCLUDING** *BEST AMERICAN POETRY*, *THE OUTLAW BIBLE OF AMERICAN POETRY*, **AND** *POSTMODERN AMERICAN POETRY: A NORTON ANTHOLOGY*. **TRINIDAD LIVES IN LOS ANGELES.**

MY SECRET LIFE

from *The Book of Rachel*

May - December 1976

If memory is a vibration, I need only meditate on that sad interlude in my life and it all
comes pouring back. I dropped out of college and moved to San Francisco
to be a real poet, or a poet in the real world. Against my parents' wishes, of course.
I can still see my mother standing behind the screen door on the front porch of the house on
Comanche Avenue, as my friend John, who was giving me a ride to the airport, pulled
away from the curb. When I spotted her silhouette, I felt a pang of guilt—as if I was
abandoning her—and burst into tears. And so began what I hoped would be a great
adventure, a launch into freedom, but would turn out to be, sadly, an Icarus descent.

Initially I stayed with a friend, Patricia, in Hayward. She'd been my manager at
Topps & Trowsers in the Topanga Mall a few years earlier—one of the part-time
jobs I had while I was in college. And one of the more boring ones: I folded and reshelved
a lot of "trowsers" that customers had tried on and discarded in the dressing rooms.
(When Pat left her job and moved to the Bay Area, she was replaced by Sheldon,
a go-getter obsessed with monthly quotas, who fired me because I wasn't an
aggressive enough salesman. One day a faded Hollywood actress, Gloria DeHaven,
came into the store with her teenage son, and I was turned off by her grandiosity.

She asked to be waited on by the manager instead. This was the last straw for Sheldon—
my mishandling of a celebrity prepared to pay big bucks.) Pat offered to put me up
until I found a job and place of my own in the city. Her house had a foresty feel:
wood-shingle facade, shaded by pine trees. The spare bedroom was upstairs, next to
her daughter's. Memory does not bring forth her name, only that she was suffering
from colitis and spent most of the time in her canopy bed. Every day I took BART
across the Bay (forty minutes each way), to job hunt and familiarize myself with
the city. (I'd spent a month in San Francisco in the summer of '73, after some gay friends
moved there from Los Angeles, so it wasn't completely foreign to me. One weekend
that August, my friends rented a houseboat on the Russian River. I shared a cabin
with an acquaintance of theirs—memory almost brings forth his name, I can feel it
hovering there—who, during the night, kept reaching for my cock. I kept pushing
his hand away. I don't know, maybe if he'd made some effort, during the day, to get
to know me. . . . The next morning, he told one of my friends that I was the only guy, in
all his years since he'd come out, who'd ever turned him down.) I had no luck
answering ads in the newspaper, so decided to try an employment agency. I could type
extremely fast, with a minimum of mistakes, and hoped to find an office job. But I lacked
experience. Recently, however, I'd held a part-time job at a small Deli in Chatsworth,
so the woman at the agency sent me on an interview to a coffee shop below Market

Street called 3 T's. A hole-in-the-wall lunch joint. The owner, Mr. Kim, liked and hired me.
And told the agency that he didn't so I wouldn't have to pay them the fee (half of
my first month's salary). Six hours a day, five days a week, at $2.75 per hour. "Should
be enough to survive," I wrote to John. During the noon rush, I made salads and sandwiches
while Mr. Kim, who turned out to be absent-minded, tried to manage the hamburgers
on the large black grill. Once he saw how capable I was, we switched positions. No one
could flip those beef patties faster than I could. His pretty young wife took care of
the cash register. And a Hispanic boy named Rick, with whom I had a brief friendship,
bussed the tables. One afternoon, while we were cleaning up after lunch, Mr. and
Mrs. Kim had an argument, which quickly escalated into a physical struggle. As Mr.
Kim dragged his wife into the walk-in freezer, she called out, "Help me, David!"
I stood frozen, didn't know what to do. Mrs. Kim didn't seem to hold this
against me, though. On several occasions after the incident, she gave me a ride
home in her white Lincoln town car. (I usually took a crowded bus to work
and, to save money, walked one mile home.) I never did learn who or what the 3 T's
were, but joked that I, Trinidad, was one of them. Naive, twenty-three, living the
poet's life in the shadow of the recently completed Pyramid Building.

Home was an apartment which I found shortly after Mr. Kim hired me, at 667 O'Farrell
Street, in the Tenderloin, a single on the second floor. Bathroom, narrow kitchen (with

breakfast nook and cloudy window that looked down on a depressing air shaft), and hallway
that opened onto what I remember as a fairly large room with a high ceiling. A wall of windows,
with sheer, diaphanous curtains, faced the back of another building. A diagonal fire
escape was also part of the view. The plaster walls had cracks and chips; the blood-red
carpeting was scarred with cigarette burns. The apartment also had cockroaches, which
I was too inexperienced and timid to complain to the landlord about. The faucet in the
sink in the bathroom had a perpetual drip. In June, soon after I'd moved in, John drove up
from Los Angeles with some of my possessions: typewriter and poems, a box of cherished
books (Anne Sexton's single volumes among them), sheets and blankets, pillows, dishes,
clothes. And copies of *The New Yorker* that had arrived since I moved. (In those days,
I subscribed and read the poems religiously. The ultimate achievement, I believed, was
to publish a poem in that esteemed magazine—an ambition I inherited from Sylvia Plath.
Today that ambition is filed away under "some dreams they forgot.") John also brought
my stereo and records. "I'm going crazy without music," I'd written in a letter.
"In my apartment all I hear is the ticking of my wind-up clock, the noisy steam-heater,
traffic in the distance, etc." John had driven up on a Friday. On Saturday, we took the ferry
to Sausalito, wandered through the shops (full of work by local artists: watercolors,
ceramics, handmade candles set in pieces of driftwood) and ate lunch at a cafe overlooking
the water. On Sunday morning, after we ate breakfast at the appropriately named David's

Delicatessen, on Geary Street between Mason and Taylor (where, for thirty-five cents,
I bought my weekly treat—a bear claw glazed with white icing and sliced almonds),
John drove us to Golden Gate Park. There he snapped a picture of me in the rose garden,
surrounded by pink "First Love" roses—a joke about my ex-boyfriend Tom, for whom I was
still carrying a torch. I'm wearing rose-tinted sunglasses and a baby blue denim jacket
I stole from Topps & Trowsers after Sheldon fired me (I didn't buy it, as I mistakenly
stated in an earlier poem), and I'm smiling at our "First Love" pun. John, who knew Tom
and thought him shallow, tried to convince me he wasn't worth it. To no avail.
In the afternoon, John left for the seven-hour drive back to Los Angeles. As soon as we
hugged and I watched his car disappear down O'Farrell Street, an acute loneliness set in.

In the following weeks, I checked out, from the public library, armloads of art and poetry
books and continued, on my own terms, my education. I read biographies of Rimbaud
and Emily Dickinson, and tore out, from the photo sections, pictures of my idols. These
I affixed, with masking tape, to the plaster wall above my twin bed. (I'd one day make amends
for these defilements by donating books to the Los Angeles Public Library.) From a monograph
on Paul Delvaux, I cut out a picture of *The Blue Sofa*. In the painting, a nude woman
reclines on a blue couch; behind her, another nude woman, draped in a red cloak, holds a
candle. On a wall: a painting within the painting: full moon presiding over the ocean. The room
is open to a nighttime scene: a cobbled street and, in the distance, a tunnel from which

a black-robed figure, carrying a lantern, emerges. All is dimly lit, and tinted blue. I loved
Delvaux's mysterious and dreamlike landscapes. I also loved the paintings of Dorothea Tanning,
which I discovered in one of the books on Surrealism I checked out. And from which I
removed a black-and-white reproduction of her *Temptation of Saint Anthony*. Alone in the desert,
the bearded saint cowers as his ragged garments fly up and hover over him, like a wave about
to break, and morph into visions of nude female bodies—breasts and bellies and buttocks.
At the same time, he is being preyed upon by naked female demons. A tableau of sexual
torment. Her other paintings, like *Eine Kleine Nachtmusik*—which depicts two young girls
whose ruffled dresses shed from them, like frilled petals, as they encounter, in a hotel hallway,
a giant sunflower—seemed to perfectly articulate the mystery and secrecy of erotic fantasies.
When I tried to write, alone in my single apartment with the ticking of the wind-up clock
and the rattling of the radiator, nothing satisfactory happened. Gone was the inspiration
I felt when I wrote my Thebes poems; I wondered if it would ever return. (Last night,
June 14, 2025, I watched a delicious Pre-Code with Jimm and Celeste: *This Modern Age*, from 1931,
starring a blonde Joan Crawford. Reunited with her mother in Paris, Joan finds herself torn
between a life of sin and a life of respectability. After Jimm retired, Celeste and I played
dominoes—with the brightly designed Jonathan Adler set that I bought in a shop on
Vermont Avenue last week—then sat and chatted, as we sometimes do. I told her about
this poem, how it came out of left field, I didn't expect to write it, at least not now, in the middle

of this book of poems about Rachel. But "way leads on to way," said Celeste,
quoting Frost.
Will it make all the difference? I told her that it's intentionally digressive,
both in the sequence
of Rachel poems and within itself. I see where I am at this point in the
narrative, sitting
in that dingy single apartment in the Tenderloin—which in the seventies
was known as
a seedy, even dangerous neighborhood, with all the bars and hucksters
trying to entice
you into strip clubs, but on some level it was the atmosphere I needed to
live out my
Rimbaud in San Francisco fantasy—and being unable to write. It's taken
a lifetime of
practice—and how many forks in the road—to fully enjoy the freedom, to
paraphrase
Robert Creeley, to say only what I want to say.) Hoping it would free me
from my block,
I paid for and attended a workshop led by Paul Mariah. At his apartment
in—was it the
Mission District? Dolores Heights? I only remember that I had to take a
bus there.
And that as it passed through a congested area—a crowd on the sidewalk
on one side,
moving slowly in front of a row of colorful shops, people sitting on the grass
on the other,
men with their shirts off, sunbathing, having animated conversations—I was
struck how
everyone seemed comfortable in their own lives, in their own skin, in a way
I was not, and
doubted that I ever would be. Mariah, well-known as a gay poet, was editor
of *ManRoot* magazine
and press. *Personae Non Gratae*, a chapbook of poems about time he spent
in prison,
had garnered him some attention. I bought a copy of it at City Lights
Bookstore; that's where I
noticed, on a bulletin board, a flyer for the workshop. I can see, in my mind's
eye, his living

room: floor-to-ceiling bookcases, plants in macrame hangers, indirect afternoon light.
A circle of seven or eight chairs. All men and one young woman. I was too intimidated to
comment on their poems. High-strung, Mariah led the group with an egotistical air of
authority, as if he fancied himself a prophet of poetry. The young woman went right before
me; Mariah heaped her poem with praise. Then I passed out copies of my offering—
a poem-in-progress based on a Greek myth—and read it with a nervous quaver.
After an uncomfortable silence, Mariah jumped up, pulled a book from a bookcase, and
proceeded to read, dramatically, Denise Levertov's "A Tree Telling of Orpheus."
A reverent hush followed his recitation. "*This* is how you write a poem about a Greek
myth," he pronounced. All eyes turned to me, naturally, to take in my reaction.
I tried to hide the fact that I felt humiliated; rather than instruct, Mariah had succeeded, for
whatever reason, in putting me in my place. I destroyed the poem as soon and I got home.
Needless to say, I did not return to the workshop. And could not think of Mariah, thereafter,
without wishing him ill. (He would die of AIDS in 1996, at age fifty-eight. By 2010,
he'd be referred to, on the internet, as a "forgotten San Francisco poet.")

To educate myself—and perhaps to punish myself as well—I found (at a used bookstore)
and read Denise Levertov's *To Stay Alive*. It didn't include the Orpheus poem that Mariah
had used to belittle me. And it didn't speak to me in a way that would have been useful
at the time—that would come several decades later, when I read her work closely and came

to appreciate her—though there were several statements in her preface to the book
that might have been instructive, had I been able to hear them, and which give me
encouragement now: that every poem is a part of a larger fabric, "a whole in which each
discrete work is a part that functions in some way in relation to all the others"; and that
a record of one's experiences can only transcend "the peculiar details" of your life by
being expressed "in and through such details." I ran across another flyer for a poetry workshop,
this time free and close to my apartment on O'Farrell Street. Despite the sting of the
Mariah workshop, I was willing (and determined even) to try again. What I encountered
was more of a social gathering: a church basement full of gay men, seated at rows of
cafeteria-style tables, and talking among themselves—a din that may as well have been
happy hour at a gay bar. I found a seat in the middle of it all. "I thought this was a writing
workshop," I said to the two guys across from me. One of them got up and walked to the
front of the room, then returned with a man named Steve. Steve had been slated to run
the workshop that night, but it had not been properly announced and no one had brought poems
with them. "I did," I said. So Steve listened—amidst the din—to me read "The Sphinx," one of
my Thebes poems (I wasn't about to risk sharing something in progress again). Involuntarily,
to ward off criticism, I admitted that I had a long way to go. "You've come a long way
already," Steve replied; he said that he thought my poem had "nice images." Just then, the guy
who'd fetched Steve appeared with a boy in tow. A tall boy, cute, nineteen (as it turned out), whose

name was Christopher. Who stood staring at me. "A *poet*," he breathed, entranced by the idea.

People appear and become part of your life. That's how it was with Christopher. We became
instant friends (not lovers) and before too long he moved into the apartment on O'Farrell Street.
Carted another twin bed and a few boxes of his belongings up the stairs to the second floor.
An escapee from a Baptist family that was never going to accept his homosexuality,
Christopher N., as he wanted to be known, was outgoing and curious about other people and
the world. Whereas I was prone to sit home and read, and try to write poems. An extrovert
to my introvert. (In some ways it was a dress rehearsal for my friendship with Rachel.)
To me he was the incarnation of Christopher Today—the Holly Golightly-esque character
in the story I'd written for a fiction workshop at CSUN. Free-spirited and hedonistic, an enfant
terrible in the making. Christopher had grown up in the East Bay and still had a job there,
working with elderly people. He'd come home in the afternoon and find me depressed—
about my job at the coffee shop, about not being able to write—and attempt to raise my spirits.
One day he appeared with a wooden fruit crate he'd picked up in the street, for me to use
as a bookcase. Another time he found an unused roll of butcher paper. On a swath of it
I printed, with a Magic Marker, Anne Sexton's "Her Kind"—one of my favorite poems—
which we hung above my bed. "I have gone out, a possessed witch, / haunting the black
air, braver at night," she writes. And repeats, at the end of each stanza, "I have been
her kind"—a reworking of Robert Frost's "I have been one acquainted with the night."

My Emily Dickinson T-Shirt

I saw a woman wearing
one and asked her where
she bought it. She told me:
at a women's bookstore
called Old Wives Tales
on Valencia Street, below
the Castro. I made a pil-
grimage: I had to have that
T-shirt. Upon entering the
store, I was told, bluntly,
by the clerk behind the
cash register, to leave: NO
MEN ALLOWED. I hadn't
noticed the sign. Hardcore
early feminist separatism.
While the men partied, the
lesbians resented. (It wasn't
until AIDS that they began
to show some alliance with
gay men.) They had other
literary T-shirts for sale:
Gertrude Stein, Jane Austen,
Virginia Woolf. Standing in
the doorway, I pleaded with
her to sell me the Dickinson.
She agreed, finally, as long as
I didn't cross the threshold.
I don't know how we con-
ducted the transaction from
a distance. But I got what I
wanted—the only time I've
ever had to beg a retailer to
sell me something—a white
T-shirt with my idol on it,

the only known photograph
of her, daguerreotype rather—
the same one I'd torn from
a library book and affixed
with masking tape to the
plaster wall above my twin
bed—taken of her in 1847,
when she was still a teen-
ager. She looks directly at
the camera, her face "as
simple and plain as a hand-
kerchief." Black crepe dress
and velvet ribbon around
her white neck, that forms
an X at her throat. Holding,
tentatively, "a white, trans-
lucent blossom." I wore it
often, an emblem of identity.
Christopher took a Polaroid
of me in it. Unfortunately,
I have a goofy, wide-eyed
expression. I lean against
the wall of windows in the
apartment. Behind me,
through the sheer, diaph-
anous curtains: darkness
of night. You can see that,
after so many washings,
Emily has begun to recede,
like a ghost I called forth
that's now taking its leave.

For a few months it was fun. I had companionship, and more money, since we split
the rent, for food, and to buy books and records with. Christopher, who dreamed of becoming
a film director, dragged me to many movies. I say "dragged," but I probably went
without much arm-twisting; I loved movies. Christopher loved horror films, the cheesier
the better; he had a camp appreciation of trash. We saw movies like *The Omen* (Damien
the Antichrist), *The Food of the Gods* (gigantic mutant wasps and rats), *It's Alive*
(murderous infant with fangs and claws), *Burnt Offerings* (gothic house as parasitic
entity, with an ancient Bette Davis), and *Eaten Alive* (in which a deranged hotel owner
feeds his guests to a monstrous crocodile that lives in a swamp). We saw *Night of*
the Living Dead, which completely unnerved me. I've never forgotten, in the scene
in the cemetery, the zombie lumbering towards the blonde woman in the trench coat,
or the scene in the basement where the little girl stabs her mother with a bricklayer's
trowel. We saw *Logan's Run* (about a futuristic city where everyone has as much sex
as they want until the age of thirty, when they're "renewed," i.e., done away with),
and revival films like *The Group* and *Sweet Bird of Youth* (I was struck by the blonde beauty of
young Shirley Knight, who appears in both). And thrillers like *Marathon Man* and *Don't Look Now*.
Christopher insisted I come with him to see a movie called *The Rocky Horror Picture Show*. This was
before it became a spectacle of audience participation; there were only half a dozen people
in the theater. We saw movies by directors we admired. Roman Polanski's *The Tenant*, which was

its own kind of horror film, and deeply upsetting: the main character,
played by Polanski,
so intent on committing suicide, he throws himself from a building twice.
We saw
Brian De Palma's *Carrie* the day it opened and were so blown away we
stayed to see it
a second time. Who wouldn't want to turn one's high school prom into a
bloodbath?
(I had no idea that the costume designer, Rosanna Norton, was the daughter
of Ann Stanford,
my poetry teacher.) De Palma, the new Hitchcock, was our new hero; we
sought out showings
of his earlier films, such as *Phantom of the Paradise* and *Obsession*. After
Christopher saw
Maîtresse at the Music Hall, French actor Gérard Depardieu became his
romantic ideal.
The movie itself sparked a significant change in him, a sudden obsession
with kink: bondage
and discipline, S & M, spike heels, torture chambers, black latex head masks,
leather whips.
I mark this as a turning point in our relationship, one that would lead us,
eventually, in
different directions. For the moment, Christopher was sleeping with the
projectionist of
the Powell Cinema, where we saw *Fellini Satyricon*. This projectionist
referred to the image
on the poster as "two nelly guys on a horse." Not the most meaningful of
memories, but one
that has hung on for half a century. Each morning, I would tell Christopher
my dreams
and he would write them down. He turned them into a script for a movie
he wanted to make:
Nine Dreams of a Poet. He got hold of a 16mm camera and we proceeded to
film them.
I remember images from two of the dreams: steam rising from a manhole
(a sight
that always fascinated me) and a nude man riding a horse. We filmed the
first late

one night, at the corner of O'Farrell and Hyde; the second, at a pasture
 somewhere outside
of the city. Christopher wanted me take off my clothes and get on a horse
 he had rented.
I refused. I didn't want to take off my clothes out there in the middle of
 nowhere.
And I was afraid of horses. So Christopher stripped, jumped on the horse,
 and galloped up
a hill. And I filmed it. The project was abandoned after that. Christopher
 was furious
because he had saved and spent money on the rental of the horse, and I
 had been "difficult."
But by then I'd decided to move back to Los Angeles, and there was tension
 in our friendship.

It was Christopher who introduced me to the Club Baths. A fifteen minute
 walk from where
we lived. Down Hyde, which turned into 8th Street below Market; the baths
 were at 8th
and Howard. You'd stand in line, pay for a locker or room at the window,
 and be handed
a small white towel and a spiral key chain that you could slip on you wrist
 or ankle.
You'd undress, wrap the towel around your waist, and then enter a dim
 labyrinth of narrow
halls, wandering dreamlike past room after room. Tiny rooms—just enough
 space for
a single bed and small table. If a guy was available, his door would be open.
 He'd be inside
naked, waiting. If you were interested, you'd lurk in the doorway, playing
 with yourself,
eyeing him; if he was interested in return, he'd give you some kind of signal,
 and you'd step
in and shut the door behind you. If a guy in one of the tiny rooms was lying
 on his stomach,
it meant he was willing to be fucked by anyone; you simply helped yourself,
 leaving the door
open so others could watch. On busy nights you could hear the beds
 squeaking in unison,

like cicadas in the heat of summer. The whole place felt steamy, and had a rank smell
of poppers and sex. You could bypass the maze altogether and make your way straight
to one of several orgy rooms, where men openly had sex with each other. The orgy room
I preferred had little cavelike cubicles, tucked away from the main action, where two people
could have some semblance of privacy. In one such cubicle I made out with a short
Mexican guy who had the biggest cock I'd ever seen. Sweat made our bodies sleek,
slippery. He kept trying to convince me to come with him, he had a room. And kept
fingering my ass, so I knew what he was after. As I'd been raped, I wasn't easily seduced.
He finally gave up and went in search of someone else to fuck. Another night, I stood,
in my skimpy white towel, against a wall in the labyrinth, impassively smoking
a cigarette. A guy walked right up to me, reached under the towel, grabbed my cock.
I liked his directness, and followed him to his room. We exchanged phone numbers
and had sex a few more times, once at his apartment, once at mine. We lived
a convenient block from one another. It was the closest I came, in my eight months in
San Francisco, to dating someone. I remember that he had soft white skin and liked
to kiss. And that we inhaled Locker Room when we came; it was worth sacrificing
a few brain cells for such an ecstatic and endless orgasm. The one time I splurged on a room
(lockers were cheaper), I lay on the narrow bed and watched the men file by in their white towels
and look me over. Few lingered; the ones who did didn't interest me enough to beckon them in.

Peter Berlin, the gay porn star with the Dutch boy haircut (I'd seen a layout of him in
After Dark, but not any of his films), stopped and leaned against the doorway. Unlike the other men,
he was dressed in his signature outfit: black mesh tank top, tight black leather pants
(that showcased his endowment), black combat boots. He stood there for what
seemed the longest time, then moved on. I was both disappointed and relieved.
Who knows what having sex with a porn star would have meant, other than having
a story that would impress Christopher. (To him, Berlin was godhead.)

I didn't fare much better at the bars. They were too crowded; it was difficult to talk
over the music, get to know someone. I did go home with one guy I met at a bar on Polk
Street. He had an apartment up the block, with a window seat that overlooked the
street. He had red hair. He had a framed movie poster of *The Yellow Rolls-Royce*,
starring Ingrid Bergman and Shirley MacLaine. What I wonder now is why that
movie was important to him. I must have been curious. Did I ask? We had brunch
in the morning, and never saw each other again. At that same bar on Polk Street,
on a frenzied Friday night, I met a guy who, I thought, resembled Gérard Depardieu
(another encounter I was sure would impress Christopher). Drunk, I told him, repeatedly,
how handsome he was. He was with his boyfriend, so we made a date to meet there
one night the coming week. I hadn't been that excited about something in quite a while.
The day of the big date, I ate a tuna fish sandwich (that I brought home from 3 T's)

and drank Johnnie Walker Red (someone had given Christopher a quart). I was already
drunk when I met the Depardieu lookalike at the bar. I remember him holding a bottle
of poppers to my nose, squeezed up against each other in the middle of the packed
dancefloor. And the next thing: the two of us starting to have sex on my single bed.
Suddenly I sat up and vomited over the side of the mattress. Then laid back down,
apologizing profusely. Nice guy: He stayed with me most of the night to make sure
I was all right. I think of this as the nadir of my time in San Francisco, if not my entire life.

Christopher also introduced me to sex in the park. Lafayette Park, in particular, at the
top of Pacific Heights, a twenty minute walk from our apartment. An uphill climb,
via Sacramento Street, tinged with the excitement of what I might find. The silent pantomime
of shadows moving in and out of the bushes, midnight rustlings, one man kneeling
before another, sucking his cock; or bending over and letting a stranger, in denim or
leather, penetrate him. It was like inhabiting a Paul Delvaux painting: fog sifting
through the tips of trees, mysterious figures traversing moonlit paths. While the city
sparkled below, like a handful of amber. Or so I romanticized. I'd given up hope
of meeting anyone to date or have a relationship with; gay life didn't seem
conducive to that. So I tried, for a couple of months anyway, to give myself over
to absolute pleasure (as Tim Curry sang in *Rocky Horror*). Only it wasn't pleasurable
at all. It was just compulsive, anonymous sex. And as I walked home from

Lafayette Park, or from the Club Baths, in the small hours, the city streets empty and silent,
steam rising from manholes—an image that haunted my dreams—I felt more
anonymous than ever. I felt like I was in one of those doomy movies Christopher dragged
me to, like there had been some sort of catastrophe, and I was the only person left in the world.

There was one romantic opportunity I might have botched. Christopher was dating
a young man named Tom. Short and boyish, whose glasses gave him a slightly nerdy
look. But cute, and docile in a puppy-doggish way. I don't remember how it came
about, but we went on a secret date. Took a bus, west on Geary, all the way out to
a neighborhood near the ocean, where he was staying in an apartment with his sister
and her husband. Walked down to the ocean, spread a blanket, shared a bottle
of red wine. When we got back to the apartment, we lay down on a couch and made out.
After we'd half undressed each other, I abruptly stood up, pulled on my clothes, and called
a taxi. Uncomfortable, I guess, because his sister and her husband were in the next room.
And feeling guilty that I was betraying Christopher. That long ride back down Geary, vacant
at dawn, I worried if I'd have enough for the fare. I didn't, and had to run up to the
apartment and borrow some change from Christopher. The next day, Tom showed up
and said, "What shall I call you now? 'Darling'?" Given what had transpired
the night before, I thought it odd, and inappropriate, and put him off. When I confessed
my deception to Christopher, he couldn't have cared less. He was done with Tom, he told me.

I regretted, long after, that I didn't at least entertain the possibility of an affair with him.

I wanted to escape, so one night I went, alone, to a science fiction double feature. Of
the two, the movie I really wanted to see was *The Time Machine*, one of my favorite films
from childhood. Handsome Rod Taylor builds a time machine and transports himself
into a future where the Eloi, young men and women, all blond and wearing pastel shifts,
are enslaved by the Morlocks, horrible mutant creatures, with blue skin and rotting teeth.
The Morlocks live underground and cannibalize the Eloi. Taylor defeats them and frees
the beautiful blond people. In order to see this favorite film, I had to sit through *Forbidden Planet*,
a movie I didn't particularly like—monsters from the id and all that. The theater was
jam-packed; the only empty seat I could find was in the front row, on the left side,
second seat from the center aisle. How it started: The guy to my right kept staring over
at me. I couldn't bring myself to turn and look him in the face, just had a sense of him
out the corner of my eye. He pressed his knee against mine. When I didn't pull away,
he reached over and began rubbing my crotch. And when he unzipped my pants I didn't
stop him; it was a fantasy I'd had since adolescence. He seemed especially interested in
my pre-cum. Self-conscious, I slid my jacket over my lap. His fondling went on until,
afraid I might come—he was getting me close—I pushed him away. He reached in his
pocket and tried to hand me a wad of cash. Offended, I quickly zipped up my jeans
and left the theater. My instant indignation—*I may be loose but I'm not a whore!*—

surprised me. And left me doubly frustrated: I didn't get to come, I didn't get to see
the movie I wanted to see. When I got home and told Christopher the story, he became
angry, and laid into me. *We could have used the money!* The fact that he didn't understand
my reaction was another indication that my San Francisco adventure was coming to an end.

As was (what turned out to be) my last sexual experience in the city. I ended up—god
knows how—at a bar in the financial district. A tourist—German? Dutch?—picked me up
as I was playing pinball and took me to his hotel. A nice hotel; I felt conspicuous as he
led me across the posh lobby. His English wasn't very good, but not much talk was
necessary. Early the next morning, as I walked down Post Street, feeling seedy among
the throng of men and women freshly dressed for a day of business, a day full of meaning
and purpose, I repeated to myself the Anne Sexton line I'd printed with Magic Marker
and hung above my bed: *I have been her kind. I have been her kind. . . .* I repeated it
as I crossed Union Square, walked one block down Powell, and turned right on O'Farrell.

Christopher N.'s Encounter with Katharine Hepburn

Katharine Hepburn
was in town to perform
in *A Matter of Gravity*
at the Curran Theatre,
a couple of blocks from
our apartment. Christo-
pher happened to be
walking on Geary Street
when he spotted her
entering the stage door.
"Miss Hepburn, I love
you!" he called out. She
turned and yelled back:
"You don't know anything."

Sullen and sunk into myself, I waited—as if my life depended on it—for Patti Smith's
second album, *Radio Ethiopia*, to come out. Christopher bought a copy at Tower Records
in North Beach the day it was released. We sat and listened to it—and were gravely
disappointed. It lacked the magic of *Horses*. Smith became, for a time, a fallen angel.
(Her third album, *Easter*, would resurrect her.) I'd come to terms with my own defeat:
My great leap into the real world of poetry had been a complete failure. After how
many months, and how many crumpled-up attempts, I had only one poem to show
for my efforts. And a bad one at that. Called "The Red Ledge." About a suicide,
a man who jumps to his death from his fourth-floor apartment (which resembled my own:

"cracks in the wall, black / cigarette burns in the carpet"). I kept it as
a souvenir of
sorts; it had an image in it I liked, of a sign above a corner bar on
O'Farrell Street,
that I'd passed numerous times: a red champagne glass that "fizzes / and
overflows in
neon consistency. / The room is tinted pink." But my literary pursuits were
not altogether
fruitless. I discovered, in an issue of *Gay Sunshine*, a poem by Dennis
Cooper,
"Rimbaud and Verlaine." The best poem I'd read thus far by another gay
poet.
(I was fed up with the mediocre paeans to blond boys that dominated the
"fag rags.")
It pointed, without my knowing it, to the future: Dennis and I would
become good
friends after the accident. And I discovered the poems of Jana Harris.
One night
I was at City Lights, downstairs in the poetry section, when a reading for
her new chapbook,
This House that Rocks with Every Truck on the Road, was about to begin. The
event was free,
so I sat in one of the folding chairs and listened. And liked her poems so
much I bought
the chapbook for $3.50, just about all I had in my pocket. (I still have my
copy with
the price, written in pencil, on the flyleaf.) I was too shy to go up to her,
but would come,
also in the years after the accident, to correspond with Harris (her
personalized
stationery was pink) and finally meet her in person. Both she and Dennis
wrote the kind
of poems I hoped to write—clean and clear, personal and lyrical, yet
unsentimental,
and unafraid to be explicit. I had a long way to go, but had found
contemporaries
I admired—a big encouragement. I began searching for their work in
literary journals.

Though he was on the cusp of becoming a hustler, Christopher was dating a Hungarian
hairdresser he'd met through his job working with elderly people. This hairdresser, whose
name was Cal, wanted Christopher to move in with him, but Christopher had no desire
to return to the suburbs he'd successfully escaped. Christopher brought Cal to our apartment
late one afternoon when I was sitting, depressed, under "Her Kind" watching the
sheer, diaphanous curtains billow in and then fall flat. They wanted me to go out with
them, but I declined. Christopher later told me that Cal had called me a "loser." This
stung, of course. And helped solidify my resolve to move back to Los Angeles. I knew—
don't ask me how—that I wasn't a loser. (I have been mindful, my whole life, never to
call anyone that. It smarts like hell. And who am I to judge what someone else might become,
or what they might go on to accomplish.) There was another, more important factor
in my decision to leave. Christopher saw a listing for an open poetry reading at a bar
across the Bay. So one Friday night, he and I and the slightly nerdy but cute Tom
and one or two other friends took BART out to Berkeley. The bar was crowded and loud.
Christopher, despite my reservations, signed me up to read. When my name was called,
I did not want to budge from my seat. Christopher prodded me. I stepped up to the microphone
on the elevated platform and started to read my Thebes poems. No one paid attention.
People talked, with raised voices, at small round tables. Behind me: the clink of glasses
and bottles, and the repeated ding of the cash register. Something—anger, most likely—

kept me going. Slowly, as I read on, the din began to diminish. By the last poem,
the entire bar was silent. I finished and stepped right down; the applause lasted until I was
back in my seat. Then the clamor resumed. I sat there astonished. *I had silenced the bar!*
There *was* something in me worth cultivating. And there was nothing in San Francisco,
that I could see, that could help me do that. Christopher believed in me; or maybe
he just liked the idea of "a poet"—the first words I'd heard him breathe. But things had
changed. He was taking a dark turn, and becoming more and more impatient with
me; he was angry that I was leaving. By Christmas, I'd be back at my parents' house
on Comanche Avenue. I'd reenroll at Cal State Northridge, take more workshops with
Ann Stanford, and begin to write poems again. And one day at school, in the cafeteria
on the roof of Sierra Hall, I'd see Rachel Sherwood sitting alone, reading *Modern Love*
by George Meredith, and—as fate would have it—sit down opposite her.

AL VANSICKLE
FROM HERE OR SOMETHING

AL VANSICKLE IS A POLITICAL ACTIVIST AND MARKETING COPYWRITER BASED IN LITTLE ROCK, ARKANSAS. A FORMER INTERN AND LATER ASSOCIATE EDITOR FOR SIBLING RIVALRY PRESS, SHE HAS ALSO ASSISTED IN ORGANIZING NO KINGS MARCHES AND CONTINUES IN THE FIGHT FOR SOCIAL JUSTICE. HER PASSIONS INCLUDE TEA BLENDS, DANCING, AND MUTUAL AID. AL LIKES TO WRITE ABOUT WHAT YOU MIGHT BE THINKING AND TO SHARE CINNAMON TWISTS WITH HER CAT, FINLEY. INSTAGRAM @HUMANINPICTURES

SHY

Rising past
witching hour
spell pulling ~
magnetic
magick, a single
press again,
again

The night
is young yet.
So is this, so
are we, too
exhilarated
to be frightened.
Fly away, lover

with my—touch—
fall together
fall apart,
nothing but warm
dust
in cotton sheets

Gasping, grasping
the morning light
from your spine,
grace of your hip,
line of your thigh
[the hour stands still]

SOMETIMES I FIT

my limbs
sideways crumpling
into my own warm

heels into
thighs into
gut.

creased into corner
whispering, *i'm sorry*
to the walls

it's been six years.

we tell ourselves
we are not that girl.
we are more then they made us

tell her
these are scales
not scars.

shed the last of me

until it is my own hands
on my throat
my own words

choke.

being angry
does me
no good, but

why is it,
i have this whole damn house
and still find myself sitting in the closet.

TWIST THE TURN

drop your glass for the rapture
nothing but sausages
pork to make them rich

we are unsettled
a wildfire in us
a riot
a dancing girl
          too much spinning no stop

we belong to the trees
the roots of us match
just the same.
so much growing to be done

the floors are cold
so we must wear socks
the earth, she calls

but this house rests on a crawl space

BURN

Do you hear them crying?
Babies with bloated bellies
float up the desert,
rock asleep to nursery bombs.

Take our labor, becomes blood
in the sand.
Take food from our mouths,
medicine from our veins.

Poison our water.
Sell it back in plastic bottles
that poison the air.
Buy that, too.

Force us to the streets.
Jail us for it.
We will not stand down.
Cut every tether to touch the light,

the love again.
Love like soft sheets,
her warm breath against our neck.
They want to take even this.

Dios mío, nos quieren quitar esto.

We were born to love
    like baked bread
        sweet milk
        handmade bouquets
        close dancing in the rain

but every day they take
and all that is left is   pits

in our stomachs
tears in our eyes
ash in our mouths

so we love like dragons
and burn it all down.

RAWHIDE

If you don't like it here then leave
only works if you've never seen
Ozark in October trees
fog dancing low 'fore first freeze

i'll be and be buried here
lungs overgrown with her mycelium
veins flooded with the creeks
swollen through my roots

dive deep and retrieve me
everything we'll come to be
all we are currently
flows back to the Mississippi

ate mud pies with the strays young
i know pack when i smell it.
nothing like sweet southern comfort
papaw´s Copenhagen and off-color jawin'

like when you give a dog a bone, but it's rawhide
rots us out from the inside
we'll find home in the right kind
tangled up with the barbed wire

right

nothing tastes quite like this
rusty oak and honeysuckle air
this is the dirt i'm made of
we, me, and the pokeweed

AUTUMN

Enter the realm of my view.
I am drawn to you.

Something in you is calling,
Turn my ear to the sound.

Loamy soil,
soft & cool against my lifelines
settled, not still
I touch touch   touch
only once more,
a harmless lie.

How did my hand
find your back?
Your neck
is tilting to me.

Bury into your eyes,
bright already,
alight now, even
fading with sleep.

A kiss to your forehead,
            each laugh line
where your lips turn up.

I tilt, too.
Somersault.
Fall.

ALMOST NO

She showed me a safer silence, morning peace,
where wild onions grow 'low the trees,

how to fish in a moving creek,
and how to love someone, but choose me.

She showed me how to look down at all my roots:
some ya foster, some ya prune,

look like a winner, but sorely lose,
how fearful I am of a burning fuse.

She showed me how to wait for more to grow,
how to play loud a little more,

how to be a stranger and all I know,
and how to let an almost go.

She sure felt like home to me,
but my mama's house kept me lonely.

That's why I moved on down the road.

My tears won't be drowning me,
but I can taste the salt when I breathe.

I'd stay here, if I knew how to float.

It could be the therapy,
or my own complex arresting me,

smelling smoke when there's ash on my nose.

And sometimes, when my memory
only sees rose history,

I have to replay the final show.

There's a lot that she taught me,
things I didn't want to need,

and how to let an almost go.

COULD I

lay you down?
Scrape my teeth along the stretch of your
neck?
Dimple sweet oil into the crevice of your
shoulder?
Lean in to catch your breaths?
Dig deeper?

You are a great plane
with your valleys and caves,
I ache to explore you
adore you
go before you—swallow you into me.

You are sweeping mountains
and how I love your climb.
Your petal thighs
spread wide
circling my mind.

Just rest, sweetheart,
release your torrent.
I'll dance in your downpour
free and yours,
press your trembling limbs
back into your skin.

LISTEN TO ME

Suck me of my marrow
fill your stomach with rot

There is more here than stars, my darling
You only just got here

Hurt me so i have a story to tell
make it good make it a good one

You nestle to my throat
calm comfortable

Got me drawlin out my words
like I'm from here or something

Hear the cicadas purr
Feel it to your toes

Check the closets, but we both know
the monster is under the bed

EAT A BURGER

Feelin cold again
The boys find it endearing
Here I am, wrap me up
Chase away this feeling

My bones jar together
Do you hear the crackling?
Call me little bird
Hear the crows cackling

Do you feel so so small?
See how they lied to me?
"Milk and meat will grow you tall"
Lactose intolerant and weak

Face to face the mirror
Do you recognize me?
Eat a burger, you'll fall over
Mediocre beauty queen

Don't you love to fit in?
I collapse upon myself
Fold at all my sharpest corners
Place me on the highest shelf

"A little loud—just shut your mouth"
Do you even know your mind?
"You're so tiny, I could lift you up
Could break you if I tried"

Face to face the window
Do you recognize me?
Eat a burger, you'll fall over
Mediocre beauty queen

Still not graceful, still too kind
Trace your veins, see them fine
Love your body baby
I'm glad to know she's mine

Face to face the door
Who are you to be?
Eat a burger, you'll fall over
Mediocre beauty queen

MATTHEW WILLIAMS
POEMS INSTEAD OF FUCKING

MATTHEW WILLIAMS IS A LIBRARIAN LIVING IN CINCINNATI, OHIO, WITH HIS HUSBAND, RYAN, AND THE GHOST OF THEIR ORANGE TABBY, ROTHKO. HE WAS FIRST PUBLISHED IN THE SHORT STORY COLLECTION *USERLANDS: NEW FICTION FROM THE BLOGGING UNDERGROUND* **EDITED BY DENNIS COOPER. HE HAS BEEN AT WORK ON HIS POETRY COLLECTION** *WALLPAPER* **FOR FAR TOO LONG.**
INSTAGRAM: @JUDGEABOOK

THE BATHROOM CHANDELIER

I wrote about forgiveness and forgetting. I wrote
about faggots and fucking. I wrote until you stopped
reading. I distracted and dissuaded the most loyal.
In the final act, I always cut away too soon. Dear reader.
I did it all for you. But there comes another stage and
a new performance. I sip the champagne slowly
because it isn't binge drinking when it is slowed
to a crawl. If I pause to scrawl prose as the spine
of my night, I can recount the history of the alphabet
just before dawn. And at dawn the cats scratch the lawns
of the sleeping neighbors while I slide back to bed.
An orator at rest is restless and lust filled. Sometimes
the sounds make more sense than the words and I don't
know why that will always break my heart. But the reminder
of humanity is good. Even if we disrobe ourselves
of certain hopes and dreams with each year. We can't live
forever in one form. So we seek another. I hope to leave whispers.

MAPPING

Where is the poem of the painted wall, of the painters,
and the paint. Where is the poem of my mother's cancer
and my father's cough? And the poem about moving
the couch to get the hidden bits of webs. How about
the poem of being fucked on a wooden table now residing
in a kitchen in Tennessee. What about the poem of
the trees in Kentucky and the wind in Colorado. I'm thinking,
maybe, I've caught a glimpse of the bend of the hand,
the turn of the wrist, the finger's flick. But where? When?
I looked for the poem detailing the dust in the grooves
of the records spun, spinning thin. I asked the poet to write
to me a poem about the rain puddle on the porch after a storm
blown sideways. I don't know if silence is refusal or work
in progress. I took notes for a poem and then asked the room
if the notes of a poem are all a poem ever was. But the waiter
just asks me if I want more tea. I agree to tea and think of the bag,
dripping, against the dish. The stain of it all. Can a poem be a list
of all the ways I've stained: clothes, carpets, teeth, friendships, the earth.
I wanted someone to write the laughter of a party as the entirety
of the prose. I asked others because someone reads them
and awaits their work. I asked others because I think the poetry
of writing a poem might be too cliché. Where is the poem that stops
the reader and the page. The poem that sets fire in the wild
and in the home. I asked for a verse crying at a concert, in an elevator,
in a room of strangers. I asked why are you crying. And I want a poem
that answers while wiping away the tears.

ARCHIVES

I have letters under my fingernails. Addressed
to men i fucked for free, for coke, for weed, for
love. I remember love was once a plan. I remember
evenings in fields of overgrown vegetables and weeds.
I. I. I remember refusing to capitalize "i" in the 8th grade
because I felt so small. And my English teacher told me
I would start getting a failing grade if I did not follow
the rules. What if I told her how many rules had been
broken against my body? What if I told her a capital I
was destroyed in the barn where the chickens screamed
and the hay made my naked body itch? What if I slapped
her face and told her that was nothing compared to
my body's memory of the lower case? I think about how
many attempts I made at truth before being told rules
and lies were all that were left. I think of my bare feet
in the dirt and the cum on the rotten wood of a barn
in the middle of Kentucky. And I remember being
told "I" does not matter. Only rules.

ON WRITING

I write to the hangovers, the hungover.
I write to the coffee stained tables, circles
unfinished. To the late night walks looking
over the shoulder for a world whispering
something better. To the remembrance
of things past. All things. I write to the last
time you cried next to a stranger and they
never knew. Sometimes it happens in a line
at the grocery store. I write to what we don't
control, can't control, and shouldn't control.
I write to the freedom of the middle of the night
when everything seems so silent and still. I write
to the blade of grass and all the other moments
making up a yard. I write to you because it gets
harder to write to myself. To remind and remember.
I write to forgive. I write to root into meaning. I write
to ask why you read. To ask what we did and will do
and have marked off as never doing again. I write
to find you less alone. I write to the morning fog of
your breath in the car. To the keys of the piano in
a house of your childhood. I write to keep you close.

FIELD NOTES ON A BATH HOUSE

I left some lies behind and folded
a few to tuck behind my ears. I
think it is in our flesh we leave a
piece of mistaken identity. We are
draped Grecian in misplaced towels.
Our backs tight to the steam room
tiles like a reptile's skin. We slither
and strut. One doesn't ask for hand
outs. But the occasional odds and
ends are presented. My therapist
would tell me I was making a huge
mistake. Luckily, every therapist
has failed me so I sit nude in the
body I don't even call my own. Just
an over washed towel across my lap
concealing nothing because this is not
about the chase. To market we go.
And they look away each time and I
am the stray kitten just licking my
wounds. Tail between my legs as the
night bubbles from hot tub jets that
push away the same way I am doing.
Have done, will do. Their erections
somehow the last and only piece of
them to keep them alive. Divining rods
but there is nothing divine here. No
table settings or sturdy nails. Just the
silent way men will always pass over.

PULLAN AVENUE

I miss late night kisses with strangers
and large crowds of unknown and
unnamed apartment parties leading
to roofs and bedrooms and spilling out
into hallways where we kiss and pass
joints and the shots are as sweet as
the flowers blooming on the vines
breaking against the brick of the old
buildings our youth will eventually haunt.
And I miss our cigarettes twisted and piled up
in the ashtray like hash marks counting down
time like it was only all going to last as long
as a pack of camels. What if it hasn't ended
and we're still pieces half dressed under the moon
while a friend calls from blocks away asking
'where am I?' and we're all so stoned we wonder
if this is something philosophical or if she's drunk
in the maze of side streets leading and leaving.
I think there are so many questions I have asked
over the years and I am still waiting for answers.
We're more patient in our youth. But now
I have aged and twisted my roots deeper into
something akin to soil. I will one day go into detail
about soil and soul. We come from one place, but
I have no idea where the fuck we're going. So
in the meantime I just keep coming. We're drunk
on fire escapes not quite escaped or on fire. We're
never one or the other. We are just always
and forever the in-between.

APOLOGY

When it wasn't the morning, it was the night before.
It was the last bits of stale, sleepy breath and the
lines of pillow creases. Creases creasing creased.
It was the morning, not the night before, and you
sat down with coffee and a notebook like it was
years earlier. I wanted to ask about the last time
you wrote, but I know I don't see hear every key
stroke. Keyboards, door keys, car keys—why
can't we hang them all on a hook in the closet
so we don't forget. How to drive, how to go home,
how to write. You used to tell me forgetting was
the easiest thing we're ever asked to do. You
said it goes beyond conveniences and grievances.
The forgetting is not the forgiving, you made clear.
There was something so beautiful in writing like
it was a first time. Was that how it worked after we
fucked for the first time in months? The completely
reimagined uses of language, body. You always
confused sex and sentences. Syntax and sin
slip from your tongue regularly. I'd find you curled
on the couch on the hottest afternoons without
much to say. And you believed in the silence more
than you believed in anything else. You would tell
me it was never meant to hurt me. I've often asked
myself about the violence of suggestion. The power
of acknowledging without addressing. A letter with
no stamp. Time and time again. But we're here
on a morning today ten years ago some time before
I knew these patterns. A muted pianist of poems.

IN CHICAGO

In Chicago, I end up writing poems
instead of fucking men. I guess there isn't
much to this fact. Both are little corners
of a personal life, not often shared. And
somehow they each inspire one another.
It's art that makes me wake and
sometimes that is a song or a painting or
a cock. There is a longing in life we can fill
with wonder. Lately, I have noticed the loss
of the tactile as in everyone just wants
more pics or won't run their fingers
over a sentence in a book or stand
so close to a painting the docent gets
nervous. I want it in my face and
at my fingertips. In my mouth: language
wrapped in the hotel sheets. Sometimes
I wander the museum hallways and scroll
the Grindr photos and forget to smile
because we've trained ourselves to believe
there is yet more. Another level of awe
waiting around the corner. But I still cry
in front of the Barnett Newman vertical
on the wall of the Art Institute. It waits all
day to remind us we're split, incomplete.

BARSTOOLS

I think we're on our fourth or fifth,
but we make the best of bodies
and mind because we rarely keep
track. We ask for the empties to
be carried off like the dreams we
drink away. If we were asked
directions to where we've been
I wonder if we'd get it right. As a
matter of fact, where have we
been? And what if we didn't treat
any of it, our bodies and the other
bodies, like secrets? It all leads
to the lies climbing the walls like
flies we just assume will die in
a corner or under the cat's paw.
We used to discuss the evenings
and how they always forgot us,
but we've started turning the
tables and leaving the little bits
of history out in the fields of our
corn-fed youth. Where we stuff
memories into scarecrows
and watch the crows scatter.

GRIN

Do you have a body worth slipping against the night
with if the photos aren't of you in the gym or a sleeve-
less T or at least four bumps across your stomach
with which we learn to read Braille and the sentence
is incomplete. Do you know how to love if you seek
a third when you're drunk or when you're sober or when
you need to remember you don't live within the lines
of rules or the bodies just want to want because
sometimes the simplest answer is the only answer. But
if you aren't judging is the faggotry of the game thrown
out the window like a burned out cigarette with a
one, two, three spark across the road. A firework
without a 401K. If the answer takes too long does the
question become the problem. A regret as recipe for
better luck next time or the next time or the next or
the time after that. Or maybe one must prep ahead
of time with a glass of champagne for the giggles and
a bit of popper for vacancy and a single hit of weed
for the body to tingle in case those fingers come up
too dry or lost. The bodies can't always be left on
their own wandering in the wreckage of sheets.

ESSEX HEMPHILL (1957–1995) was one of the most celebrated Black gay poets of his generation. Hemphill's first collections of poems were self-published books, including *Earth Life* (1985) and *Conditions* (1986). He edited the Lambda Literary Award-winning anthology *Brother to Brother: New Writings by Black Gay Men* (1991). His first full-length collection, *Ceremonies: Prose and Poetry* (1992), won the National Library Association's Gay, Lesbian, and Bisexual New Author Award. He died on November 4, 1995, of AIDS-related complications. In 2025, New Directions published his *Love Is A Dangerous Word: Selected Poems.*

BRYAN'S POEM

This issue, I wanted to give my space to Essex Hemphill for the final word. Here's his poem "The Perfect Moment," published with permission of New Directions and the Estate of Essex Hemphill.

ESSEX HEMPHILL

THE PERFECT MOMENT

for Robert Mapplethorpe

Aesthetics can justify desire,
but desire in turn
can provoke punishment.
Under public scrutiny
the eyes of one man
are focused on another.
Is it desire, equality,
disgust, or hatred?
Is the quality of loneliness
present or overlooked?
Is it diminished
by the breaking of taboos?
Is the passion mutual
or is one wary of
the other?
Does fear haunt the edges
of the photographs?
Does it blaze inside the cornea
or lurk like men in shadows
posed for the perfect moment
to snap or strike or sigh?

www.ingramcontent.com/pod-product-compliance
Lightning Source LLC
LaVergne TN
LVHW052340100826
845147LV00021B/1134

* 9 7 8 1 9 4 3 9 7 7 8 9 5 *